T0185608

The Advanced Game Developer's Toolkit

Create Amazing Web-based Games with JavaScript and HTML5

Rex van der Spuy

Apress®

The Advanced Game Developer's Toolkit: Create Amazing Web-based Games with JavaScript and HTML5

Rex van der Spuy
TORONTO, Ontario, Canada

ISBN-13 (pbk): 978-1-4842-1098-7   ISBN-13 (electronic): 978-1-4842-1097-0
DOI 10.1007/978-1-4842-1097-0

Library of Congress Control Number: 2017945373

Cover image designed by Freepik

Managing Director: Welmoed Spahr
Editorial Director: Todd Green
Acquisitions Editor: Louise Corrigan
Development Editor: James Markham
Technical Reviewer: Tom Barker
Coordinating Editor: Nancy Chen
Copy Editor: Karen Jameson
Artist: SPi Global

Distributed to the book trade worldwide by Springer Science+Business Media New York, 233 Spring Street, 6th Floor, New York, NY 10013. Phone 1-800-SPRINGER, fax (201) 348-4505, e-mail orders-ny@springer-sbm.com, or visit www.springeronline.com. Apress Media, LLC is a California LLC and the sole member (owner) is Springer Science + Business Media Finance Inc (SSBM Finance Inc). SSBM Finance Inc is a **Delaware** corporation.

For information on translations, please e-mail rights@apress.com, or visit http://www.apress.com/rights-permissions.

Apress titles may be purchased in bulk for academic, corporate, or promotional use. eBook versions and licenses are also available for most titles. For more information, reference our Print and eBook Bulk Sales web page at http://www.apress.com/bulk-sales.

Any source code or other supplementary material referenced by the author in this book is available to readers on GitHub via the book's product page, located at www.apress.com/9781484210987. For more detailed information, please visit http://www.apress.com/source-code.

Printed on acid-free paper

Contents at a Glance

Contents

About the Author

Rex van der Spuy is a leading expert on video game design and interactive graphics, and he is the author of the popular Foundation and Advanced series of books about how to make video games. Rex has designed games and done interactive interface programming with Agency Interactive (Dallas), Scottish Power (Edinburgh), DC Interact (London), Draught Associates (London), the Bank of Montreal and TVO (Canada). He's also built game engines and interactive interfaces for museum installations for PixelProject (Cape Town, South Africa), and built "Ga," the world's smallest full-featured 2D game engine; and its full-featured sister engine, "Hexi." He created and taught advanced courses in game design for many years at the Canadian School of India (Bangalore, India). The highlight of his career was programming video games on the Annapurna glacier at 4,500 meters (which, to his delight, was 1,000 meters higher than the maximum permissible operating altitude of his laptop). Rex spends his free time sleeping, and tuning his sitar.

About the Technical Reviewer

Tom Barker is a husband, father, engineer, technical leader, professor, author, amateur classicist, aspiring winemaker, and maser. Currently, he is Senior Director of Software Engineering and Development at Comcast.

Acknowledgments

In Chapters 2 and 3, the walking elf character was based on graphics designed by Wulax (opengameart. org/content/lpc-medieval-fantasy-character-sprites), and forest background graphics were based on tiles designed by Leonard Pabin (opengameart.org/content/whispers-of-avalon-grassland-tileset).

The heart, skull, and marmot graphics were designed by Matt Hackett (`https://opengameart.org/users/richtaur`) and score a perfect 5/5 Tigerhats. Go Lost Decade Games! `http://www.lostdecadegames.com`.

The isometric cubes in Chapter 4 were by author GameArtForge (`https://opengameart.org/content/isometric-cubes-set-01`).

CHAPTER 1

■ ■ ■

Getting Started

Welcome to the HTML5 game designers toolkit! This book is an essential guide to the most useful techniques you need to know for making a wide range of 2D action games. It covers classic development practices, tools, algorithms, and architectures, including the following:

- How to use Tiled Editor to design game levels (Chapter 2).

- Efficient collision detection using tile-based techniques (Chapter 3).

- Designing isometric game maps and collision detection in isometric games (Chapter 4).

- Pathfinding for maze games, including line-of-sight and A Star (Chapters 5 and 6).

- The amazing efficiency of tile-based games, and some surprising things you can do with them (Chapter 7).

These are all the techniques you need to know to create almost any kind of game in any genre.

What You Need to Know

You're a game designer! And, you need to have a reasonable fluency with JavaScript and HTML5 technologies. If you're reading this book, you've already made a few games and have a toolset or game engine that you're happy using. You know how to make sprites, run a game loop, test for collisions, write game logic, and handle user input. You should also have some familiarity with vector math: how to calculate vectors, normalize them, and create new vectors from other vectors.

■ **Note**   If you don't know any of those things, or need a refresher, pick up a copy of *Foundation Game Design with HTML5 and JavaScript* (Apress, 2012), *Advanced Game Design with HTML5 and JavaScript* (Apress, 2015), and *Learn PixiJS* (Apress, 2015). These three books will teach you everything you need to know.

This book is completely agnostic about which technology you use to make games. The source code has been written in JavaScript using a simple 2D HTML5 game engine called Hexi. However, the code examples are purely intended to be a kind of psuedo-code that you can apply to any other programming language or game engine. It doesn't matter what game engine or display list framework you use – you can apply the concepts in this book to any of them. The important things about the code in this book are the algorithms, the high-level concepts, and the code comments – not necessarily the implementation details. I'll leave those up to you, for whatever technology you choose.

© Rex van der Spuy 2017

R. van der Spuy, *The Advanced Game Developer's Toolkit*, DOI 10.1007/978-1-4842-1097-0_1

All you need to do is make sure that the technology you're using has a full hierarchical scene graph (also known as a display list). That means you're able make sprites and nest them as children of parent sprites. And, your technology needs some way of letting you reference the following properties on your game sprites (values are in pixels, unless stated otherwise):

> **gx**: The global horizontal position of the sprite, relative to the game screen's top left corner.
>
> **gy**: The global vertical position of the sprite, relative to the game screen's top left corner.
>
> **x**: The local horizontal position of the sprite, relative to the sprite's parent's top left corner.
>
> **y**: The local vertical position of the sprite, relative to the game screen's top left corner.
>
> **width**: The sprite's width.
>
> **height**: The sprite's height.
>
> **halfWidth**: Half the sprite's width.
>
> **halfHeight**: Half the sprite's height.
>
> **scaleX**: The sprite's horizontal scale (as a normalized value between 0 and 1).
>
> **scaleY**: The sprite's vertical scale (as a normalized value between 0 and 1).
>
> **centerX**: The sprite's center x position.
>
> **centerY**: The sprite's center y position.
>
> **rotation**: The sprite's angle of rotation, in Radians.
>
> **alpha**: The sprite's transparency (as a normalized value between 0 and 1).
>
> **vx**: The sprite's vertical velocity.
>
> **vy**: The sprite's horizontal velocity.
>
> **layer**: The sprite's position in the display stack (0 is the bottom layer).

You'll also need some way to group sprites together into a parent container, and some functions to help you manage this:

> **group**: Groups sprites into a parent container.
>
> **addChild**: Add sprite as child of another sprite or container.
>
> **removeChild**: Remove a sprite from its parent sprite or container.

These are the only sprite properties and functions you need to make any kind of 2D game you can think of. Although the names will likely be different, any 2D game development tool you're using will let you access these properties and functions in some way. Just identify them in the tool that you're using, and you'll be able to make use of the code in this book.

Hexi and Ga

Most of the source code in this book has been written using a minimalist 2D HTML5 game engine called Hexi. It's been designed, by me, as a tool for making the widest possible range of games while writing the least amount of code. You can find out all you need to know about Hexi, including detailed tutorials and examples, here:

github.com/kittykatattack/hexi

If you have any questions about the specific implementation of the code in this book, refer to that link. (The source code in this book is based on Hexi v.0.1).

Hexi also has a little sister, called Ga.

github.com/kittykatattack/ga

Ga's API is the same as Hexi's but the code base is almost 10 times smaller. How is that possible? Because it uses an extremely lightweight canvas-based renderer, without WebGL. In fact, Ga was specifically written so that its core could compress down to less than 6.5k, making it an appropriate tool to use to for micro-gaming competitions, like the annual JS13K event (js13kgames.com). It's also a great way to learn about low-level graphics rendering, without having to deal with the often unnecessary complexities of WebGL.

If you want to know the inner details of how Hexi or Ga works, or want to build your own custom game engine from scratch, you'll find everything you need to know in this book's companion, *Advanced Game Design with HTML5 and JavaScript*. Ga is really just a production-grade version of the code developed in that book. And Hexi is just an implementation of the same API with a PixiJS-based (WebGL) renderer running under-the-hood.

The Source Code

You'll find all the source code for this book here:

github.com/kittykatattack/agdt

The code is organized into chapters. Just clone the repository, launch a web server in the root directory, and open the examples in your favorite browser.

All the example code has been written in the latest version current of JavaScript: ES6/7 (also known as JavaScript 2016/17.) This code was written at a time when these standards were so new that no browser vendor had yet fully implemented them. If you're in that same position, I suggest you use a JavaScript ES6 transpiler, like Babel (babeljs.io) to compile the ES6 source code into production-ready ES5. In all the source code example files, you'll find a folder called src that contains the ES6 source, and a folder called bin, which contains the transpiled ES5.

CHAPTER 2

■ ■ ■

Using Tiled Editor

If there's only one piece of software that every game developer should learn how to use, it's Tiled Editor (www.mapeditor.org). Tiled Editor is an industry-standard open source application that lets you easily create a visually complex layout, and then export that layout as a JSON data file that you use to build your game world. Because Tiled Editor just outputs data, it works just as well for making games with any technology, like C#, Java, or Objective-C, as it does for JavaScript. And it's not just for games – you can use it whenever you need to design a complex layout that would be difficult or time consuming to describe with code.

In this chapter we're going to take a detailed look at how to use Tiled Editor so that you can start using it with your own projects quickly. You'll find out how to:

- Prepare your source images.

- Configure Tiled Editor.

- Use Layers and Objects.

- Understand the JSON data output.

- Import the JSON data into your game code and use it to create sprites.

- Create a camera to follow a game character around a large scrolling game world.

The small effort that it takes to learn how use Tiled Editor and import its data is well worth the massive productivity boost it will give you.

We're going learn how to use Tile Editor by making a useful little RPG (Role Playing Game) engine, shown in Figure 2-1. Run the fantasy.html file in the chapter's source files to try out the finished prototype. Use the arrow keys to walk the elf character around the world and collect three items: a heart, a skull, and a marmot (which is kind of like a fat, furry Guinea pig).

© Rex van der Spuy 2017
R. van der Spuy, *The Advanced Game Developer's Toolkit*, DOI 10.1007/978-1-4842-1097-0_2

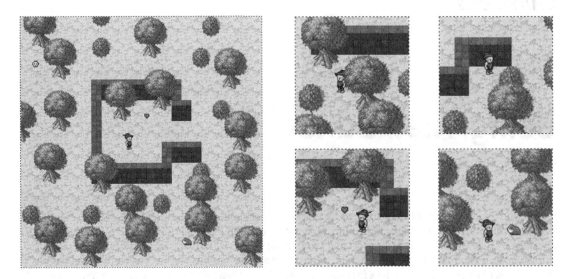

Figure 2-1. *Help the elf collect items in the game world*

All the game objects are correctly depth layered, and although the walls, trees, and bushes block the elf's path, he can walk around them as if it were a real 3D space. Creating a complex layout like this would be quite difficult if you were plotting the positions and depths of the objects using pure code – so this is the perfect job for Tiled Editor!

Choosing Your Images

The first place to start is with a tileset that contains the graphics for your game.

■ **Note**   Tilesets, also known as spritesheets, are just single images that contain all your game images as sub-images.

You'll need to create your game graphics using a graphics editor like Illustrator, Pixelmator, Photoshop, Gimp, or Piskel and then package them with a tool like Shoebox or Texture Packer.

The entire scrolling game world was built using only the small handful of images shown in Figure 2-2. The finished game world looks complex, but it only took a few minutes to snap together using this tileset. Most of the sprite images are 64 x 64 pixels, but the smaller ones on the top right are 32x32. The big tree is 128x128 pixels. You can mix and match sprites images of any sizes, although you'll make life much easier for yourself if you keep them to sizes that are powers of 2 (8x8, 16x16, 32x32, etc.).

Figure 2-2. *Start with a tileset*

You can see that the tileset contains all the sprites in the level except for one: the elf character. That's because we're going to add the animated elf later - directly in our game code. (You'll see how in the steps ahead).

Making a Map

A **map** is the name that Tiled Editor gives to the game screen layout that you're creating. It's just a rectangular grid of cells. The game map that we're creating in this chapter is a 24 by 24 grid of cells, with each cell being 32 pixels wide and high. That means the entire map has a width and height of 768 pixels.

To create a new map in Tiled Editor, select File ➤ New from the menu. The New Map dialogue box will appear to let you set the map's properties, as shown in Figure 2-3. Select **orthogonal** orientation for a flat, 2D map. Choose CSV layer format so that the map information will be output as arrays. Also, keep the Tile render order's default value of Right Down. Then set the width and height of the map, in tiles, and then define the width and height of each tile. If you have a tileset with different sized images, set the tile height and width to the size of the *smallest* image. In this example, the smallest images on the tileset are 32x32 pixels. Select OK when you're done.

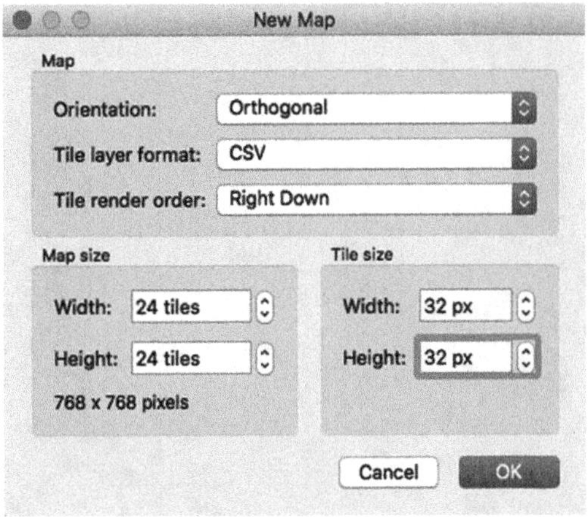

Figure 2-3. *Set the map properties*

■ **Note**   In this book I've use Tiled Editor version 0.15.0, which was the latest at the time of writing. The version you're using will likely have a slightly different organization, layout, and output, so just treat these details as a general guide and use your own judgment about how to apply them.

Next, load in your tileset. Click the New Tileset button in the Tilesets panel on the right-hand side of Tiled Editor's workspace. Give your tileset a name and set the Type as "Based on Tileset Image." Browse to the tileset's location, and define the height and width of each tile. Again, set this height and width to the size of your smallest sprite image. In this example, I've named the tileset "fantasy," and set the tile width and height to 32 pixels, as shown in Figure 2-4. If your tileset has spacing (padding) around each image, enter the spacing amount here. (Tilesets produced by software like Texture Packer adds two pixels of default padding around each tileset sub-image). Click OK when you're done.

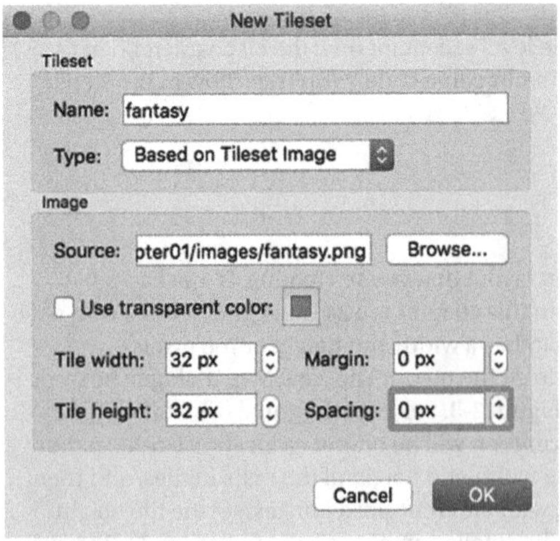

Figure 2-4. *Set the tileset*

■ **Note**   You can use more than one tileset for each level if you need to, and the tilesets can be any size. Instead of using tilesets, you can optionally build your game using individual images files by choosing the Type option "**Based On Collection of Images**." This makes Tiled Editor an extremely flexible layout tool.

When this is done, you'll see your tileset loaded into the Tilesets panel, as shown in Figure 2-5.

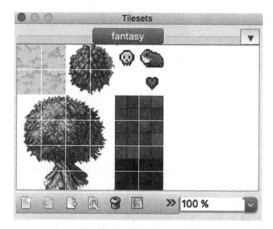

Figure 2-5. *Load your tileset*

Setting Images Properties

You can create and set properties for each image on your tileset, and you'll be able to access all those properties in your game code. In this example, I want to assign names to the skull, heart, and marmot images. Here's how to assign a name to each image:

1.   Click on an image, and find the Custom Properties section of the Properties panel.

2.   Create a new property called "name," and give the image a name.

I've named each of these images "skull," "marmot," and "heart," as shown in Figure 2-6. Later in this chapter you'll see how you can access this information as object properties in your game code.

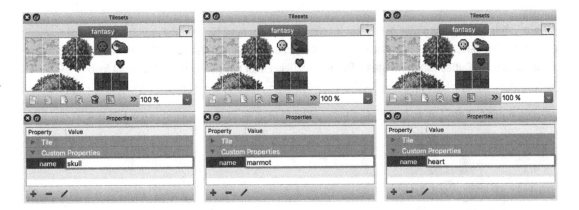

Figure 2-6. *Set optional image properties*

Using Layers

You're now ready to start building the map! Tiled Editor lets you create **layers** into which you can organize different elements of your game world. In a simple map, you might have a layer called maze that contains all the walls of your maze, and another layer called enemies that contains all the enemies in your game. The map we're building in this example is a little more complex in that we're using layers to help us create a shallow 3D effect. Our map uses six layers, starting from the ground, and working up, vertically, to the treetops:

- **ground**: The grass. This layer is for things under the elf's feet.

- **obstacles**: The bottom parts of the of the trees, the bottom parts of bushes, and the bottom parts of walls. These are things that are above the elf's feet, but below its head.

- **items**: The heart, skull, and marmot. These things are also around middle height.

- **objects**: The elf. It's also at middle height, but it should be displayed in front of the items.

- **wallTops**: The tops of the walls. These are above the elf's head.

- **treeTops**: The tops of the trees. These are above the tops of the walls.

Figure 2-7 shows a scene from the game where you can see all these depth layers at the same time. Can you match each layer with its representation in the final scene? Do you notice that the things in top layers are covering the things in the bottom layers?

6 depth layers

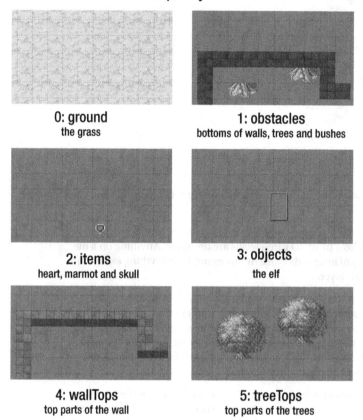

0: ground
the grass

1: obstacles
bottoms of walls, trees and bushes

2: items
heart, marmot and skull

3: objects
the elf

4: wallTops
top parts of the wall

5: treeTops
top parts of the trees

Figure 2-7. *All the sprites that make up this scene have been organized into 6 depth layers*

■ **Note**   This pseudo-3D effect is sometimes called 2.5D. It's as though you're sitting on a chair, looking down at the tabletop where the game is happening. The sprites themselves are flat, like pieces of paper, but they appear closer to us if they're near the bottom of the screen, and farther away if they're near the top.

By organizing our layers according to depth, from bottom to top, it's going to be easy to create the illusion of depth. The sprites that are closer to the viewer will overlap the ones that are farther away.

Create these six layers by clicking the New Layer button in the Layers panel, shown in Figure 2-8.

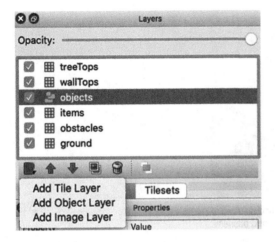

Figure 2-8. *Create some map layers*

You can see from the New Layer button menu that there are three types of layers that you can create: Tile, Object, and Image layers.

- **Tile Layer**: Use rectangular tiles to compose these kinds of layers. This is great for fixed grid layouts, which is how most 2D game levels are designed. Anything on a tile layer will end up as an array of image id codes. In this example, everything except the elf has been created on a Tile layer.

- **Object Layer**: Use this for sprites that should be placed freely and not fixed into a rigid grid system. Its also useful for placing objects that aren't in the current tileset, or which will be generated later by code. You could also use an object layer for adding non-visual game elements that provide some useful data in your game. Anything on an Object layer will be described as a JavaScript object in the final JSON file. In this example, the elf character will be on an object layer.

- **Image Layer**: Use this to position a single image. Use the Image field in the Layer Properties panel to browse for the image or set its URL. When you export the map as a JSON file, this information will generate a path to the image file along with its x and y pixel coordinates.

■ **Note**   By using object and image layers, Tiled becomes a very flexible visual layout editor for any type of game, not just tile-based ones. There are no rules about how many layers you need, the size and shape of the sprites, or what kind of things should be on each layer type. Just use whatever organization system makes sense to you for the kind of game you're making.

We're now ready to start designing the map.

Building the Map

We'll start from the bottom-most layer, the ground, and work our way up.

Select the ground layer, click on the grass tile, and use the paint bucket tool to cover the level with grass, as shown in Figure 2-9.

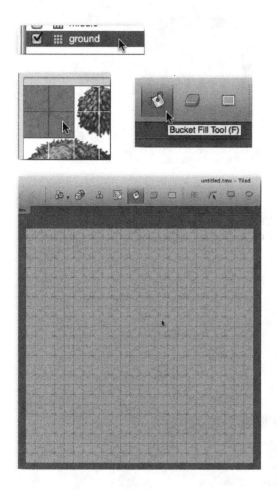

Figure 2-9. Fill the level with grass using the paint bucket tool

Next is the obstacles layer. These are the things that will prevent the elf character from moving. You can think of anything on the obstacles layer as the walls of a maze. This includes the trunks of trees, the bottom parts of the walls, and the bottom parts of the bushes.

Hold down the command or ctrl key to select more than one tile image at a time. Choose the Stamp tool, and use it to stamp sprite images onto the level. Fix any mistakes with the Eraser. See Figure 2-10.

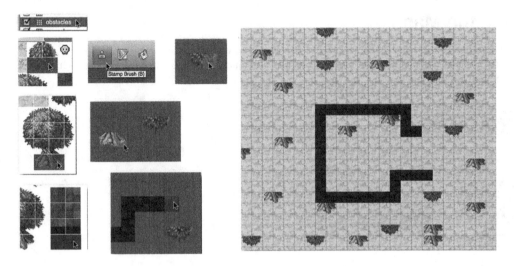

Figure 2-10. *Add the obstacles*

Next, add the items layer. These are things that the elf is going to be able to pick up. We only need three things on the items layer: the heart, the skull, and the marmot. Add these to the layer using the stamp tool, as shown in Figure 2-11.

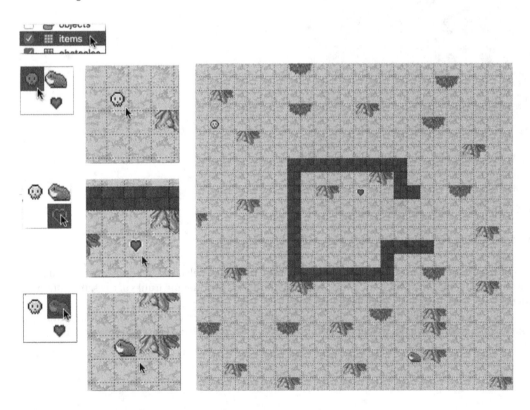

Figure 2-11. *Add the collection items*

Next is the object layer. This is where we're going to add the elf character - *as a data object*. The elf isn't represented as an image in the tileset because we're going to build it later from code as a complex animated sprite. You could use a simple placeholder image of an elf and just add it to the map in the same way I've added the other images, but instead I want to use this as an opportunity to show you how Tiled Editor's objects work.

You can see from Figure 2-12 that the layer type that the elf is on is called objects. This is a special kind of layer that lets you place things freely without snapping them to the grid. It also lets you assign a custom height and width to the object. That means you can place objects of any size with precise x and y screen coordinates. Things on object layers will be represented as an array of JavaScript objects in the exported JSON file, and you can give each object a unique set of properties.

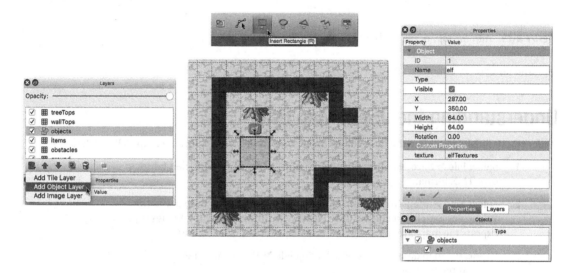

Figure 2-12. *Add an object and give it some properties*

To add something to an Object Layer, use one of the shape tools and draw the shape onto the spot where you want the object to appear. The context-sensitive Properties panel will display the properties for the new object you're creating. Tiled Editor's objects have some default properties, like position and size, which closely match properties on the sprite objects that we've been using in this book. For this example, I've set the object's name to "elf," and set its width and height to 64 pixels. You can change or add as many other properties as you like, all of which you'll be able to access in your final game code. Any object you create like this you can access from Tiled Editor's handy Objects panel.

There are two more layers to add: the wallTops and the treeTops, as shown in Figure 2-13.

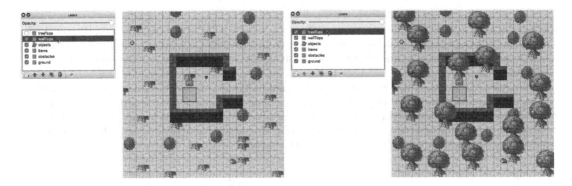

Figure 2-13. *Add the tops of the walls and the tops of the trees*

And now you're done!

Understanding the JSON Map Data

When you've finished building the map, follow these steps to save and export the map as JSON data:

1. Select File ➤ Save As... from the main menu to save the file in Tiled Editor's own TMX format.

2. Select Map ➤ Map Properties... Find the Tile Layer Format property in the Properties panel, and choose CSV. The CSV (Comma Separated Values) option exports the map layer as arrays of numbers, which is what we want.

3. Export the map data to JSON by selecting File ➤ Export As... and choose JSON as the file type.

4. We've now got a JSON file full of potentially useful map data, but how can we use it?

It's important to remember that each layer in the map is represented as an array. That means the JSON file will contain at least six arrays. Five of those arrays are full of tileset frame id codes. One of them, the one that represents the objects layer, is an array of objects. The JSON file also gives you information about the height and width of the map, tiles, and all the tile properties. All of this extra information is contained in sub-objects with their own sub-arrays. There's a lot of data, and if you open the JSON data file for the first time, you might become overwhelmed by what you see. Don't let it intimidate you! You'll soon see that the structure is quite logical and, once you understand it, it will be easy for you to use all this data in your game program.

■ **Note** Tiled Editor's data output has become a de facto standard in the game design industry, so learning how it's structured and how to incorporate it with your own games is a good long-term skill investment.

Let's keep things simple and first take a look at the broad structure of the JSON file - from a safe distance. Here's an abridged version that shows you the most important properties.

```
{
//The map's properties
"backgroundcolor": "#ffffff",
"height": 24,
"nextobjectid": 2, //Only used by Tiled Editor for internal use
"orientation": "orthogonal",
"properties": {/* Any custom properties you might have set */},
"renderorder": "right-down",
"tileheight": 32,
"tilewidth": 32,
"version": 1,
"width": 24,

//The `layers` property is an array of objects. Each object contains
//another array that represents that layer's map data. The layer
//objects also contains the layer properties, which includes
//its name, type and size
"layers":[
  {"data": [1, 2, 1, 2, 1, 2, ...], //Layer properties...},
  {"data": [0, 0, 0, 0, 0, 0, ...], //Layer Properties...},
  {"data": [0, 0, 0, 0, 0, 0, ...], //LayerProperties...},
  {"objects": [{"name":"elf", //...more object properties...}], //LayerProperties...},
  {"data": [0, 0, 0, 0, 0, 0, ...] ], //LayerProperties...},
  {"data": [19, 20, 21, 22, 0, ...], //LayerProperties...},
],

//The `tilesets` property is an array of objects. Each object
//represents one of the tilesets used in the map. (We only used
//one in this example.) These objects contain default tileset
//properties, and also custom properties, like the sprite image name
"tilesets":[
    { //...Tileset properties, like the width and height of each tile.
      //The custom tile name properties that we set:
      "tileproperties": {
        "11": {"name": "heart"},
        "4": {"name": "skull"},
        "5": {"name": "marmot"}
      },
    }
  ]
}
```

Most of map data, the stuff that actually tells you what's in each cell of the map, is in the "data" property of each layer object. Let's take a look at the first layer object and see what's inside:

```
{
  "data":[
      1,2,1,2,1,2,1,2,1,2,1,2,1,2,1,2,1,2,1,2,1,2,1,2,
      7,8,7,8,7,8,7,8,7,8,7,8,7,8,7,8,7,8,7,8,7,8,7,8,
      1,2,1,2,1,2,1,2,1,2,1,2,1,2,1,2,1,2,1,2,1,2,1,2,
      7,8,7,8,7,8,7,8,7,8,7,8,7,8,7,8,7,8,7,8,7,8,7,8,
      ...etc.
     ],
   "height": 24,
   "name": "ground",
   "opacity": 1,
   "type": "tilelayer",
   "visible": true,
   "width": 24,
   "x": 0,
   "y": 0
},
```

You can see that it contains some useful properties, like the layer's name and its type. The data array is a list of 576 numbers that represent all the tiles on that layer (24x24 tiles = 576). The numbers are called the **grid id**, or **gid**, and each one refers to an image in the tileset. Tiled Editor numbers each tileset image from left to right, starting from 1. Figure 2-14 shows how the grid id's of the first 12 tileset images. You can see that 1, 2, 7, and 8 match the grass tiles. The data array uses these numbers to represent the visual layout of each layer.

```
[
 1,2,1,2,1,2,1,
 7,8,7,8,7,8,7,
 1,2,1,2,1,2,1,
 7,8,7,8,7,8,7,
 1,2,1,2,1,2,1,
 7,8,7,8,7,8,7
],
```

```
[
 1,2,1,2,1,2,1,
 7,8,7,8,7,8,7,
 1,2,1,2,1,2,1,
 7,8,7,8,7,8,7,
 1,2,1,2,1,2,1,
 7,8,7,8,7,8,7
],
```

Figure 2-14. *Grid id numbers are used to represent sprite images in an array*

In our map we created five tile layers and one objects layer. The objects layer has an array called objects that contains just one object in this example: the elf. You can see that all the properties we assigned to the elf, like its name and size, are accessible as an object in this array.

```
{
 "draworder": "topdown",
 "height": 24,
 "name": "objects",
 "opacity": 1,
 "type": "objectgroup",
 "visible": true,
 "width": 24,
 "x": 0,
 "y": 0,
```

19

```
"objects":[
  {
    "height": 64,
    "name": "elf",
    "properties": {/* Any custom properties */},
    "rotation": 0,
    "type": "",
    "visible": true,
    "width": 64,
    "x": 287,
    "y": 350
  }]
}
```

Finally, there's an array called tilesets that represents all the tilesets we used to build this level. Each tileset is represented as an object, and we only used 1 in this example:

```
"tilesets":[
  {
    "columns": 6,
    "firstgid": 1,
    "image": "../images/fantasy.png",
    "imageheight": 192,
    "imagewidth": 192,
    "margin": 0,
    "name": "fantasy",
    "properties": {/* Any custom properties */},
    "spacing": 0,
    "tilewidth": 32
    "tileheight": 32,
    "tileproperties": {
      "11": {"name": "heart"},
      "4": {"name": "skull"},
      "5": {"name": "marmot"}
    }
  }
]
```

You can see that the custom name property we assigned to the heart, skull, and marmot are in the tileproperties sub-object. Notice that their id numbers are 1 less than the grid id numbers in the tileset.

■ **Note**   There is some logic to why these numbers are off by one, but you'll only appreciate this if you're using more than tileset to make a map. If you are, read on! The Id numbers used in the "tileproperties" are what Tiled Editor calls the "local" id numbers of the tiles in the tileset. These local ids start numbering from 0. The ids used in the data arrays are "global" tile ids. These global ids can span several tilesets. That means the first tileset might start its grid id numbering at 1, the second tileset might start at 32, and the third might start at 96 (0 is reserved for "no tile"). You can use the "firstgid" property of each local tileset to figure out from which tileset the global id should be. You can then map it to a local id in that tileset by subtracting the "firstgid." But if you're just using a single tileset, just subtract 1, since that's the "firstgid" of the first tileset. Confused? Don't worry! This will only start to make sense when you create your first map using more than one tileset.

Is all this data starting to make sense to you now? If you're like me, your little programmer's heart will be bursting with glee! That's because you know this is all really juicy stuff. You can use all this data to make all your sprites and lay out your game map automatically. Now how can we sink our teeth into it?

Using JSON Data to Build the Level

The JSON data doesn't know or care what kind of game we want make with it, or what technology you're using. You can use the same data to make games with Objective-C, Haxe, Unity, or Elm. That means you need to write a function that interprets this data and decides how it should be used to construct a game level. It's entirely up to you what to do with it.

Deciding How to Use the Data

Where do you start? Come up with a list of rules about how to interpret all this data, depending on the kind of game you want to make. For the fantasy role playing game that I want to make, I came up with these requirements:

- The entire game world is going to be contained inside a single **container group** called world. A "container group" is just my term for an object that contains nested child **sprites**. (Sprites, as you'll recall, are just interactive images that the game world is made from).

- Each Tileset Layer should also be its own separate group, inside the world container. There are five Tileset layers, and that means I'll end up with five groups: ground, obstacles, items, wallTops, and treeTops. All these layers have a name property, so I'll assign that name property to the layer group so that I can access it later.

- Anything on an Object layer should be returned to the game as a simple JavaScript object. I can then decide later how to use the data in that object. I'm going to use the Object's name property to access it if I need it. There's only one object in our current example: the elf.

- All the images inside the layers will be created as sprites.

- I need some way to reference all the objects that I'm creating in the world. I'm going to add two search functions that will let me retrieve objects by searching for them by name. `world.getObject("name")` will retrieve a single object that matches the name property of the object I'm looking for. It could be a sprite, layer group, or data object. `world.getObjects("elf," "obstacles," "marmot")` returns an array of objects with names that match those in the arguments.

- To keep things as simple as possible, I'm going to limit myself to one tileset per map.

This is the list of requirements that I came up, but yours might be different depending on what kind of game you're making to how much flexibility you need.

The Game Code API

Before we look at how to implement these rules, let's see what our API will look like when we're done. I'll be able to create a new game world like this:

```
let world = makeTiledWorld(data.json, tileset.png);
```

The world will then magically appear, exactly as I designed it in Tiled Editor. If I want to retrieve a layer group, sprite, or object from the world, I can do it like this:

```
let elf = world.getObject("elf");
```

I can retrieve a collection of objects as an array like this:

```
let items = world.getObjects("heart", "skull", "marmot");
```

If I have many sprites that share the same tileset name property, I can also retrieve all of them in an array. For example, if I have a tileset image with the name "wall," and I use that image 20 times in the world, I can retrieve all the wall sprites in a single array like this:

```
let walls = world.getObjects("wall");
```

This is a simple API that will be enough to give me as much flexibility as I'll need for most types of games. So how can I make all this happen?

Writing the makeTiledWorld Function

I can do all this by writing a single function called makeTiledWorld. All the details about how the code works are in the comments, but I'll highlight a few important features after the code listing.

■ **Note**   This code listing represents how makeTiledWorld is implemented by the Hexi game engine, and there are a few specific implementation details you should know. Container and Sprite are PixiJS objects. Pixi's resource loader is used to load the JSON file. (Hexi uses PixiJS as its lower-level rendering engine and asset loader). The frame function is a custom function built into the Hexi engine that captures a rectangular sub-image from a single parent image. You will need to find equivalents for these details in whatever technology you're using.

```javascript
makeTiledWorld(jsonTiledMap, tileset) {

  //Get a reference to the JSON file
  let tiledMap = PIXI.loader.resources[jsonTiledMap].data;

  //Create a container group called `world` to contain all the layers, sprites
  //and objects from the `tiledMap`. The `world` object is going to be
  //returned to the main game program after this `makeTiledWorld`
  //function finishes
  let world = new Container();

  //Set the width and height of each tile that makes up the map.
  //(The tile size is 32x32 pixels in this example)
  world.tileheight = tiledMap.tileheight;
  world.tilewidth = tiledMap.tilewidth;

  //Calculate the `width` and `height` of the world, in pixels
  world.worldWidth = tiledMap.width * tiledMap.tilewidth;
  world.worldHeight = tiledMap.height * tiledMap.tileheight;

  //Get a reference to the world's height and width in
  //tiles, in case you need to know this later (you will!)
  world.widthInTiles = tiledMap.width;
  world.heightInTiles = tiledMap.height;

  //Create an `objects` array to store references to any
  //named objects in the map. Named objects all have
  //a `name` property that was assigned in Tiled Editor
  world.objects = [];

  //The optional spacing (padding) around each tile
  //This is to account for spacing around tiles
  //that's commonly used with texture atlas tilesets. Set the
  //`spacing` property when you create a new map in Tiled Editor
  let spacing = tiledMap.tilesets[0].spacing;

  //Figure out how many columns there are on the tileset.
  //This is the width of the image, divided by the width
  //of each tile, plus any optional spacing thats around each tile
  let numberOfTilesetColumns =
    Math.floor(
      tiledMap.tilesets[0].imagewidth
      / (tiledMap.tilewidth + spacing)
    );

  //Loop through all the map layers
  tiledMap.layers.forEach(tiledLayer => {

    //Make a container group for this layer and copy
    //all of the layer properties onto it
    let layerGroup = new Container();
```

```
Object.keys(tiledLayer).forEach(key => {

  //Add all the layer's properties to the group, except the
  //width and height (because the container group will work those our for
  //itself based on its content).
  if (key !== "width" && key !== "height") {
    layerGroup[key] = tiledLayer[key];
  }
});

//Translate Tiled Editor's `opacity` property to the Container's
//equivalent `alpha` property
layerGroup.alpha = tiledLayer.opacity;

//Add the group to the `world`
world.addChild(layerGroup);

//Push the group into the `world`'s `objects` array
//So you can access it later
world.objects.push(layerGroup);

//Is this current layer a `tilelayer`?
if (tiledLayer.type === "tilelayer") {

  //Loop through the `data` array of this layer
  tiledLayer.data.forEach((gid, index) => {
    let tileSprite, texture, mapX, mapY, tilesetX, tilesetY,
        mapColumn, mapRow, tilesetColumn, tilesetRow;

    //If the grid id number (`gid`) isn't zero, create a sprite
    if (gid !== 0) {

      //Figure out the map column and row number that we're on, and then
      //calculate the grid cell's x and y pixel position
      mapColumn = index % world.widthInTiles;
      mapRow = Math.floor(index / world.widthInTiles);
      mapX = mapColumn * world.tilewidth;
      mapY = mapRow * world.tileheight;

      //Figure out the column and row number that the tileset
      //image is on, and then use those values to calculate
      //the x and y pixel position of the image on the tileset
      tilesetColumn = ((gid - 1) % numberOfTilesetColumns);
      tilesetRow = Math.floor((gid - 1) / numberOfTilesetColumns);
      tilesetX = tilesetColumn * world.tilewidth;
      tilesetY = tilesetRow * world.tileheight;

      //Compensate for any optional spacing (padding) around the tiles if
      //there is any. This bit of code accumlates the spacing offsets from the
      //left side of the tileset and adds them to the current tile's position
```

```
if (spacing > 0) {
  tilesetX
    += spacing
    + (spacing * ((gid - 1) % numberOfTilesetColumns));
  tilesetY
    += spacing
    + (spacing * Math.floor((gid - 1) / numberOfTilesetColumns));
}

//Use the above values to create the sprite's image from
//the tileset image. The custom `frame` method captures the
//correct image from the tileset
texture = frame(
  tileset, tilesetX, tilesetY,
  world.tilewidth, world.tileheight
);

//I've dedcided that any tiles that have a `name` property are important
//and should be accessible in the `world.objects` array

let tileproperties = tiledMap.tilesets[0].tileproperties,
    key = String(gid - 1);

//If the JSON `tileproperties` object has a sub-object that
//matches the current tile, and that sub-object has a `name` property,
//then create a sprite and assign the tile properties onto
//the sprite
if (tileproperties[key] && tileproperties[key].name) {

  //Make a sprite
  tileSprite = new Sprite(texture);

  //Copy all of the tile's properties onto the sprite
  //(This includes the `name` property)
  Object.keys(tileproperties[key]).forEach(property => {
    tileSprite[property] = tileproperties[key][property];
  });

  //Push the sprite into the `world`'s `objects` array
  //so that you can access it by `name` later
  world.objects.push(tileSprite);
}

//If the tile doesn't have a `name` property, just use it to
//create an ordinary sprite (it will only need one texture)
else {
  tileSprite = new Sprite(texture);
}
```

```
    //Position the sprite on the map
    tileSprite.x = mapX;
    tileSprite.y = mapY;

    //Make a record of the sprite's index number in the array
    //(We'll use this for collision detection, which you'll
    //learn in the next chapter)
    tileSprite.index = index;

    //Make a record of the sprite's `gid` on the tileset.
    //This will also be useful for collision detection later
    tileSprite.gid = gid;

    //Add the sprite to the current layer group
    layerGroup.addChild(tileSprite);
    }
  });
}

//We're now done with the tile layers, so let's move on!

//Is this layer a Tiled Editor `objectgroup`?
if (tiledLayer.type === "objectgroup") {
  tiledLayer.objects.forEach(object => {

    //We're just going to capture the object's properties
    //so that we can decide what to do with it later

    //Get a reference to the layer group the object is in
    object.group = layerGroup;

    //Push the object into the world's `objects` array
    world.objects.push(object);
  });
  }
});

//Search functions

/*
`world.getObject` and `world.getObjects` (with an "s") search for and return
any sprites or objects in the `world.objects` array.
Any object that has a `name` property in
Tiled Editor will show up in a search.
`getObject` gives you a single object, `getObjects` gives you an array of objects.
`getObject` returns the actual search function, so you
can use the following format to directly access a single object:
sprite.x = world.getObject("anySprite").x;
sprite.y = world.getObject("anySprite").y;
*/
```

```
  world.getObject = objectName => {
    let searchForObject = () => {
      let foundObject;
      world.objects.some(object => {
        if (object.name && object.name === objectName) {
          foundObject = object;
          return true;
        }
      });
      if (foundObject) {
        return foundObject;
      } else {
        throw new Error("There is no object with the property name: " + objectName);
      }
    };

    //Return the search function
    return searchForObject();
  };

  world.getObjects = objectNames => {
    let foundObjects = [];
    world.objects.forEach(object => {
      if (object.name && objectNames.indexOf(object.name) !== -1) {
        foundObjects.push(object);
      }
    });
    if (foundObjects.length > 0) {
      return foundObjects;
    } else {
      throw new Error("I could not find those objects");
    }
    return foundObjects;
  };

  //That's it, we're done!

  //Finally, return the `world` object back to the game program
  return world;
}
```

(You can find the full, working code for makeTiledWorld in the tileUtilities module of Hexi's src folder in this chapter's source files).

This code works by looping through all the arrays in the JSON data, and using that information to make sprites and and plot them in world. But there's an important detail to point out. Each sprite has been created with two new properties: index and gid.

```
tileSprite.index = index;
tileSprite.gid = gid;
```

index is the array position number of the sprite in the map array. gid is the grid id number of the sprite's texture image on the tileset. Both of these properties are going to be very useful for collision detection later, and you'll find how in Chapter 3. Stay tuned!

Now let's find out how to use makeTiledWorld to build a game.

Creating the Game World

Take a look at the fantasy.js file in the chapter's source files for a working example of a game of the game world we've created. Figure 2-15 compares the final rendered map on the left with the original map we designed in Tiled Editor.

 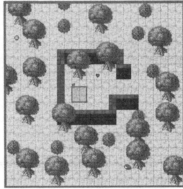

Figure 2-15. *The rendered game world matches the map we designed in Tiled Editor*

Use the keyboard arrow keys to make the elf walk around the game world, and you'll notice that the sprites are also correctly depth layered. Let's find out how the makeTiledWorld function was used to construct this scene.

Creating the Sprites

When the game code's setup function runs, the world is created from the JSON file and tileset image using makeTiledWorld.

```
world = g.makeTiledWorld(
    "maps/fantasy.json",
    "images/fantasy.png"
);
```

This generates the map, and lets us access all the map data through an object called world.

The animated elf character is created using another tileset image called walkcycle.png that contains all the elf's animation frames, as shown in Figure 2-16.

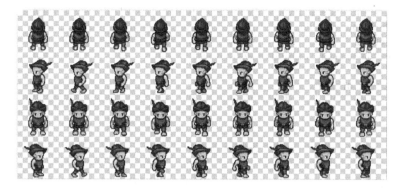

Figure 2-16. *The elf's animation tileset*

Here's the code in the game's setup function that uses this animation tileset to create the elf sprite.

```
elf = g.sprite(g.filmstrip("images/walkcycle.png", 64, 64));
```

The custom filmstrip function captures each 64 by 64 pixel frame in the walkcycle tileset and uses it to initialize the sprite.

You'll remember that in Tiled Editor we just created a placeholder object to represent the elf, and used it to set the elf's x and y position. What we want to do next is use those values to position our new elf sprite. The getObject method that we added to the world object is able to extract anything from the map data that has a name property. Here's how you can use getObject to capture the elf's x and y map data values, and apply them to the sprite's x and y position properties.

```
elf.x = world.getObject("elf").x;
elf.y = world.getObject("elf").y;
```

This new elf sprite isn't part of the world yet, so add it to the world's objects layer. First get a reference to the objects layer, and then use addChild to add the elf to it.

```
let objectsLayer = world.getObject("objects");
objectsLayer.addChild(elf);
```

The rest of the game moves and animates the elf. It also implements collision detection, and you'll learn all about how that works in the next chapter.

Changing the Sprite's Depth Layer

The elf can walk behind and in front of the trees and wall, and there's no other depth-sorting code required to make sure this works properly. How is that possible? Because the PixiJS renderer that's running behind the scenes displays sprites created last, in front of those created first. Most 2D renderers work the same way. And, because we created the sprites starting with the bottom-most layer, the ground, and worked our way up, the sprites in Tiled Editor's upper layers render in front of those on the lower layers. It all happens automatically, thanks to the careful way we planned the layers when we designed them using Tiled Editor, and the order in which we created the sprites in the makeTiledWorld function.

But what if you want to change a sprite's depth layer, while the game is in progress? For example, maybe the elf discovered a ladder somewhere and was able to climb on top of the wall. How you could display the elf above the wall but below the treetops?

Get a reference to the "treeTops" layer group and add the elf to it.

```
world.getObject("treeTops").addChild(elf);
```

Figure 2-17 shows the result.

Figure 2-17. *Change the sprite's depth layer*

Now that we've got a big game world to explore, let's add the scrolling camera.

A Scrolling World Camera

Our game map is much bigger than the game screen that it's being displayed in. But, you'll notice that it scrolls very naturally to follow the elf wherever it goes. In this section you'll learn how this scrolling game camera was implemented so that you can use these concepts to build a similar camera for your own games.

But before we find out how it was made, let's first take a quick look at the high-level game code you'll need to write to create and use the camera. First, initialize the camera in a game world like this:

```
camera = g.worldCamera(world, world.worldWidth, world.worldHeight, anyCanvasElement);
```

The first argument is an sprite with x, y, properties. The second two arguments define the width and height of the game world, in pixels. The last is the canvas HTML element that the world is being rendered in.

The camera object has two useful methods that you can use to control it: centerOver and follow. You can make the camera center itself over a sprite using the centerOver method, like this:

```
camera.centerOver(sprite);
```

Use the following method to make the camera follow any sprite inside a game loop like this:

```
function gameLoop() {
  camera.follow(sprite);
}
```

The camera has an invisible inner boundary, which is half the canvas size. You can see this invisible inner boundary on the first image of Figure 2-18. A sprite can move freely within this boundary and the camera won't start moving until the sprite crosses it. The camera will stop moving when it reaches the edge of the map, but the sprite is free to walk all the way. Figure 2-18 illustrates all these features, which results in a natural looking scrolling effect.

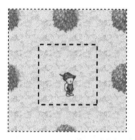
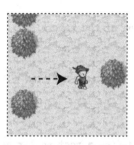
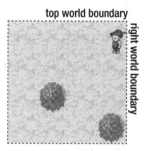

The camera doesn't move if the sprite is inside the inner boundary.

The camera follows the sprite if the sprite moves past the edge of the inner boundary.

The camera stops moving when it reaches the world boundary.

Figure 2-18. *A scrolling game camera that lets a sprite move freely around the game world*

You can think of the camera as a kind of invisible sprite that hangs over the world. It has an x and y position, and a height and width. The camera has a method called follow that changes the camera's x and y coordinates to keep up with any sprite that it's following, and a method called centerOver that centers the camera over any sprite. It also checks its position in relation to the size of the map, so that it stops itself if it reaches the map edges.

Here's the complete worldCamera function that does all this.

```
worldCamera(world, worldWidth, worldHeight, canvas) {

  //Define a `camera` object with helpful properties
  let camera = {
    width: canvas.width,
    height: canvas.height,
    _x: 0,
    _y: 0,

    //`x` and `y` getters/setters
    //When you change the camera's position,
    //they shift the position of the world in the opposite direction
    get x() {
      return this._x;
    },
    set x(value) {
      this._x = value;
      world.x = -this._x;
    },
```

```
  get y() {
    return this._y;
  },
  set y(value) {
    this._y = value;
    world.y = -this._y;
  },

  //The center x and y position of the camera
  get centerX() {
    return this.x + (this.width / 2);
  },
  get centerY() {
    return this.y + (this.height / 2);
  },

  //Boundary properties that define a rectangular area, half the size
  //of the game screen. If the sprite that the camera is following
  //is inside this area, the camera won't scroll. If the sprite
  //crosses this boundary, the `follow` function ahead will change
  //the camera's x and y position to scroll the game world
  get rightInnerBoundary() {
    return this.x + (this.width / 2) + (this.width / 4);
  },
  get leftInnerBoundary() {
    return this.x + (this.width / 2) - (this.width / 4);
  },
  get topInnerBoundary() {
    return this.y + (this.height / 2) - (this.height / 4);
  },
  get bottomInnerBoundary() {
    return this.y + (this.height / 2) + (this.height / 4);
  },

  //The code next defines two camera
  //methods: `follow` and `centerOver`

  //Use the `follow` method to make the camera follow a sprite
  follow: function(sprite) {

    //Check the sprites position in relation to the inner
    //boundary. Move the camera to follow the sprite if the sprite
    //strays outside the boundary
    if(sprite.x < this.leftInnerBoundary) {
      this.x = sprite.x - (this.width / 4);
    }
    if(sprite.y < this.topInnerBoundary) {
      this.y = sprite.y - (this.height / 4);
    }
    if(sprite.x + sprite.width > this.rightInnerBoundary) {
      this.x = sprite.x + sprite.width - (this.width / 4 * 3);
    }
```

```
      if(sprite.y + sprite.height > this.bottomInnerBoundary) {
        this.y = sprite.y + sprite.height - (this.height / 4 * 3);
      }

      //If the camera reaches the edge of the map, stop it from moving
      if(this.x < 0) {
        this.x = 0;
      }
      if(this.y < 0) {
        this.y = 0;
      }
      if(this.x + this.width > worldWidth) {
        this.x = worldWidth - this.width;
      }
      if(this.y + this.height > worldHeight) {
        this.y = worldHeight - this.height;
      }
    },

    //Use the `centerOver` method to center the camera over a sprite
    centerOver: function(sprite) {

      //Center the camera over a sprite
      this.x = (sprite.x + sprite.halfWidth) - (this.width / 2);
      this.y = (sprite.y + sprite.halfHeight) - (this.height / 2);
    }
  };

  //Return the `camera` object
  return camera;
};
```

(You'll find the worldCamera function in hexi/src/modules/gameUtilities/src/ gameUtilities.js).

You can see that the camera is really just a data model that's used to figure out which part of the world should be visible on the canvas. The camera compares its size and position against the sprite that it's following and the edges of the world.

The trick is that the camera never actually moves. When you change its x and y position, it's actually shifting the position of the world by the inverse amount.

```
set x(value) {
  this._x = value;
  world.x = -this._x;
},
set y(value) {
  this._y = value;
  world.y = -this._y;
},
```

This makes the camera look like as if it's moving around in the world, when in fact it's moving the world in the opposite direction.

Summary

Tiled Editor is one of the most useful software tools a game designer can learn. You've learned how to set up game maps; import tilesets; and use Tiled Editor's layers, objects, and tools to design your game worlds. You've also learned how to read Tiled Editor's JSON map data, and use that data to build reusable code for making a wide range of different games. And, you found out how easy it is to correctly depth layer the game objects, and add a camera that can follow a game character all around the world.

But, we're not done yet! You'll notice that in the demo game in this chapter that when the elf character walks around the world, its path is blocked by trees, bushes, and walls. And, the elf can pick up objects in the world. How does that work? You'll find out in the next chapter, when to take a detailed look at collision detection for tile-based games.

CHAPTER 3

Tile-Based Collision

There are two main ways that you can check for collisions in games. The first is to compare the x and y pixel positions of sprites on the screen. If their shapes are overlapping, you have a collision. This is a collision detection strategy called **narrow-phase collision**. If you've used a game engine with collision functions that might have names like `hitTestRectangle` or `hitTestCircle` to check whether shapes are overlapping, it's likely that these are narrow-phase collision functions. They use vector math (linear algebra) to figure out if the shapes of the sprites are overlapping. Because of that you can achieve very precise pixel-level collision accuracy, which is very important for physics-based action games.

The other way to check for collisions is to use the tile-based approach. A **tile-based collision** system doesn't use geometry to check for a collision. All it does is read a sprite's index number in an array. If a sprite is at an array map location that is already occupied by another sprite, you have a collision. For example, if a sprite is at the same location on the map as a wall, then you know the sprite is touching the wall. You can then set up some kind of collision reaction, like preventing the sprite from moving.

Note   Tile-based collision is a type of **broad-phase collision**, which you'll learn more about in Chapter 6.

A big advantage to tile-based collision is that you don't have to check every object against every other object whether they're colliding, and you don't have to do any geometry calculations. Instead, you just read an array. This makes it much more CPU efficient than a narrow-phase collision test. What's more is that you can set just a few general collision checks for different types of things, like "walls," "enemies," or "items." Even if you have hundreds of these things on a map, you just need to run one collision check for each type. This makes tile-based collision great for huge game maps that could contain hundreds of similar things. And because tile-based collisions work by reading map arrays, you can use the information about the sprite's location on the map, and its local environment, for AI or other game logic.

The disadvantage to tile-based collision is that it doesn't give you pixel-level accuracy. But it turns out that for many or most kinds of 2D action games, precise pixel-level collision just isn't necessary. Tile-based collisions have a particular "feel" to them: solid, and predictable, like you're playing a proper video game. The entire 8-bit and 16-bit video game revolution of the '70s and '80s was founded on tile-based collision, and it's still the most important video game collision technique you need to know.

Note   Do you want pixel-level accuracy, but also tile-based efficiency? You can have the best of both worlds by first checking for a collision using the tile-based approach. Then, if you detect a general collision, use a second narrow-phase test for further pixel-level precision. You'll find out how to do that in Chapter 6.

© Rex van der Spuy 2017
R. van der Spuy, *The Advanced Game Developer's Toolkit*, DOI 10.1007/978-1-4842-1097-0_3

In this chapter you're going to learn about the fundamentals of tile-based collision using some classic maze game examples. You'll get a chance to see how you can use Tiled Editor to build a flat 2D video game environment, and how to use map arrays to analyze that environment. We'll also build a general-purpose collision function for tile-based games. And finally, we'll apply all these new skills to our fantasy RPG game prototype from Chapter 2.

Understanding Tile-Based Collision

Here are the basics you need to know to do a tile-based collision. Before you start, your sprites need a new property called index:

playerSprite.**index**

The index is just a number that tells you the location of the sprite in the map array.

To find this number you have to convert the sprite's center x and y screen position into its matching array index number. Here's a general purpose getIndex function you can use to do this:

```
getIndex(x, y, tilewidth, tileheight, mapWidthInTiles) {

  //Convert pixel coordinates to map index coordinates
  let index = {};
  index.x = Math.floor(x / tilewidth);
  index.y = Math.floor(y / tileheight);

  //Return the index number
  return index.x + (index.y * mapWidthInTiles);
};
```

The next step is to find out what other things in the game world might be at that same location. For example, imagine that you have a map array that contains the location of enemies. You could call it enemyMapArray.

```
enemyMapArray = [0, 0, 0, 5, 0, 0, 5, 0, /*...*/];
```

Any location with an enemy is signified with the number "5." Any location without an enemy has it signified with "0." These numbers are called **grid index** id numbers, or **gid** for short.

You can find out which gid is at the playerSprite's location like this:

```
gid = enemyMapArray[playerSprite.index];
```

If that gid number is "5" then you know that the playerSprite is at the same location as an enemy. A collision has occurred!

```
if (gid === 5) {

  //Collision!
}
```

You now know that the playerSprite has hit an enemy. But which one has it hit?

To figure this out, your game needs an array that stores references to all the enemy sprites:

```
enemySprites = [enemySprite1, enemySprite2, enemySprite3, /*...*/ ];
```

Each of these sprites also needs an `index` property that tells you their location in the `enemyMapArray`:

```
enemySprite1.index = 52;
enemySprite2.index = 3;
enemySprite3.index = 108;
//...
```

To find the enemy sprite at the player's location, loop through the array of `enemySprites` and find the one that has the same index number as the `playerSprite`. That will be the one that the `playerSprite` is colliding with.

```
if (gid === 5) {
  enemySprites.some(enemy => {
    if (playerSprite.index === enemy.index) {

      //You've found the colliding enemy sprite!
    }
  });
}
```

These are the basics of tile-based collision, and next we'll find out how to implement them in a game.

Collecting Items

Let's look at a really practical example to demonstrate this. Run the simpleCollision.html file, shown in Figure 3-1, and use the keyboard arrow keys to help the alien character collect bombs. Each time the alien collects a bomb, the bomb disappears from the map. The message output tells you the alien's screen x and y position, and also its current map index number.

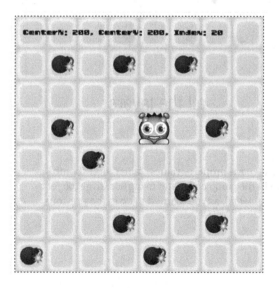 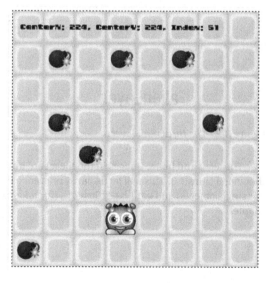

Figure 3-1. Item collection using tile-based collision

Designing the Game World

In Chapter 2 you learned how to use Tiled Editor to help you quickly design a game world. I made all example game prototypes in this chapter using the very same techniques. I used three layers: `backgroundLayer`, `bombLayer`, and `alienLayer`, shown in Figure 3-2.

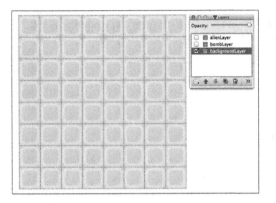

backgroundLayer

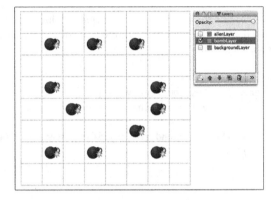

bombLayer

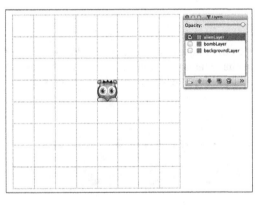

alienLayer

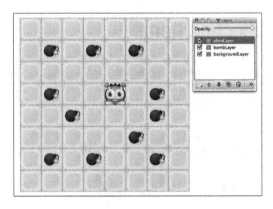

all the layers

Figure 3-2. *The three map layers*

The alien and bomb images in the tileset are both given name property values: "alien" and "bomb," as shown in Figure 3-3. This will let us easily reference them in the game code later using `world.getObject` (for single objects) and `world.getObjects` (for an array of objects), as you learned to do in the previous chapter.

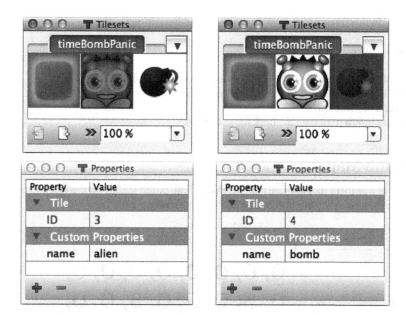

Figure 3-3. *Give names to the alien and bomb images*

Initializing the Game World

The game code loads the tileset image and also the JSON file produced by Tiled Editor. The setup function creates the world using makeTiledWorld.

```
world = g.makeTiledWorld(
  "maps/simpleCollision.json",
  "images/timeBombPanic.png"
);
```

This plots the sprites and layers on the canvas. Anything in Tiled Editor that we assigned a name property is accessible in the world.objects array. We can get references to these objects by name by using world.getObject (for single objects) or world.getObjects (with an "s," for an array of objects). Here's how to get a reference to the alien sprite.

```
alien = world.getObject("alien");
```

Our game also needs to reference the bomb layer so that we can access its data array.

```
bombLayer = world.getObject("bombLayer");
bombMapArray = bombLayer.data;
```

bombLayer is now a container that contains all the bombs as child sprites. bombMapArray is now a useful array that tells use the grid positions of all the bombs in the world. (Bombs in the array will have a gid number of 5).

We also need an array of all the bomb sprites, so we can grab them from the world like this:

```
bombSprites = world.getObjects("bomb");
```

world.getObjects searches through the world's objects array and finds anything with the name property "bomb." In this example, "bomb" matches all 11 bomb sprites in the world. bombSprites is now an array that contains references to each of these sprites.

Now let's find out how to use the bomb map data to check for collisions.

Understanding the Bomb Map

The bombMapArray is a useful array of numbers that matches the position of the bomb sprites on the screen. You can see this illustrated in Figure 3-4. Each "5" is a bomb, and each "0" is an empty cell.

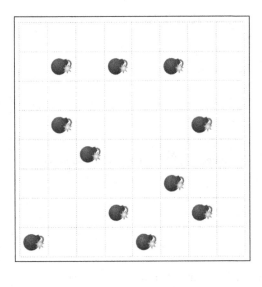

```
[
0, 0, 0, 0, 0, 0, 0, 0,
0, 5, 0, 5, 0, 5, 0, 0,
0, 0, 0, 0, 0, 0, 0, 0,
0, 5, 0, 0, 0, 0, 5, 0,
0, 0, 5, 0, 0, 0, 0, 0,
0, 0, 0, 0, 0, 5, 0, 0,
0, 0, 0, 5, 0, 0, 5, 0,
5, 0, 0, 0, 5, 0, 0, 0
]
```

Figure 3-4. An array of bombs that matches the bomb layer in Tiled Editor

When the bomb sprites are created, each new sprite is given its own index property. The index property stores the bomb's initial position in this array.

We need to know whether the alien character is in the same location as a bomb on the map. To do this we have to convert the alien's center x and y screen coordinates to its matching array index number. We can do this with the help of the getIndex function.

```
alien.index = getIndex(
  alien.centerX, alien.centerY,
  world.tilewidth, world.tileheight, world.widthInTiles
);
```

To figure out if the alien is touching one of the bombs, check to see if the alien's index number matches a bomb gid number ("5") in the map of bombs.

```
//Find out if the alien's position in the bomb array matches a bomb gid number
if (bombMapArray[alien.index] === 5) {

  //If it does, filter through the bomb sprites and find the one
  //that matches the alien's position
  bombSprites = bombSprites.filter(bomb => {

    //Does the bomb sprite have the same index number as the alien?
    if (bomb.index === alien.index) {

      //If it does, remove the bomb from the
      //`bombMapArray` by setting its gid to `0`
      bombMapArray[bomb.index] = 0;

      //Remove the bomb sprite from its container group
      g.remove(bomb);

      //Filter the bomb out of the `bombSprites` array
      return false;
    } else {

      //Keep the bomb in the `bombSprites` array if it doesn't match
      return true;
    }
  });
}
```

You can see that if the alien and a bomb share the same index number, they must be occupying the same map location. In that case, the bomb is erased from the level's bomb map by setting the gid number for that location to zero.

```
bombMapArray[bomb.index] = 0;
```

The bomb sprite is then removed from the game using a function called remove.

```
g.remove(bomb);
```

The game code is actually maintaining a live map of all the bombs in the game. Play the game, pick up a few bombs, and check the level's bombMapArray, which you see output in the console. You'll notice that each time a bomb is picked up, the cell's gid value is set to "0." The bombs were erased from the map. Figure 3-5 shows what the map's bombMapArray looks like after a few of the bombs have been picked up. You can see that it's a perfect match with the location of the bombs on the screen.

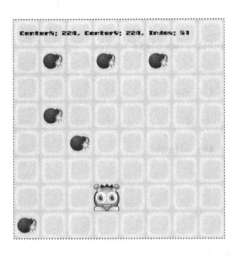

```
[
0, 0, 0, 0, 0, 0, 0, 0,
0, 5, 0, 5, 0, 5, 0, 0,
0, 0, 0, 0, 0, 0, 0, 0,
0, 5, 0, 0, 0, 0, 0, 0,
0, 0, 5, 0, 0, 0, 0, 0,
0, 0, 0, 0, 0, 0, 0, 0,
0, 0, 0, 0, 0, 0, 0, 0,
5, 0, 0, 0, 0, 0, 0, 0
]
```

Figure 3-5. When a bomb is picked up, its gid in the map gid number is set to zero

Having this kind of data updated in an array is useful for doing all sorts of other game logic analysis, as you'll see ahead.

Moving the Alien in Alignment with the Grid

Before we continue our discussion of tile-based collision, let's quickly take look at how the alien character's movement system works. Like many maze game characters, the alien moves in exact alignment with the map's grid cells. That means that when you press a key to change its direction, the alien won't move in the new direction until it's entered a new row or column in the grid. This ensures that it will cleanly transition into new rows and columns. It helps keep your collision detection system simple and dependable.

How can you figure out if a game character is exactly aligned to a map grid cell? By checking to see if the sprite's x and y screen coordinates are evenly divisible by the width and height of the map's tiles. Here's the classic snippet of code that checks for this.

```
if(Math.floor(sprite.x) % world.tilewidth === 0

&& Math.floor(sprite.y) % world.tilehieght === 0) {

    //Yes, the sprite is aligned to the map's rows and columns
}
```

You also need to ensure that the sprite has a velocity that's evenly divisible by the `tilewidth` and `tileheight`. That ensures the sprite will actually have pixel positions that allow for the above check to become true. What this means is that if your tile width and height is 64, your sprite's velocity must be a number that divides evenly into 64: 1, 2, 4, 8, 16, or 32. If the sprite has velocities like 5, 7, or 11, they'll never divide evenly into 64, and so the sprite will never become exactly aligned to the maps' rows or columns.

Here's how this works in this example. The `setup` function creates the keyboard key object that responds to arrow keypresses. A property called `direction` is then created on the alien, and the keypress actions change the value of that direction.

```
//Create the keyboard objects
leftArrow = g.keyboard(37);
upArrow = g.keyboard(38);
rightArrow = g.keyboard(39);
downArrow = g.keyboard(40);
```

```
//Create a `direction` property on the alien
alien.direction = "";
```

```
//Assign key `press` actions that change the alien's `direction`
leftArrow.press = () => alien.direction = "left";
upArrow.press = () => alien.direction = "up";
rightArrow.press = () => alien.direction = "right";
downArrow.press = () => alien.direction = "down";
```

When any of the arrow keys are pressed, alien's direction will be changed to: "up," "down," "left," or "right." The game loop checks this at each frame, and changes the alien's velocity accordingly:

```
if(Math.floor(alien.x) % world.tilewidth === 0
&& Math.floor(alien.y) % world.tileheight === 0) {
  switch (alien.direction) {
    case "up":
      alien.vy = -4;
      alien.vx = 0;
      break;
    case "down":
      alien.vy = 4;
      alien.vx = 0;
      break;
    case "left":
      alien.vx = -4;
      alien.vy = 0;
      break;
    case "right":
      alien.vx = 4;
      alien.vy = 0;
      break;
  }
}
```

The game loop then moves the alien and keeps it inside the canvas boundary using a custom function called contain.

```
alien.x += alien.vx;
alien.y += alien.vy;
g.contain(alien, g.stage);
```

> ■ **Note** It's especially important to be aware of map boundaries for any game that depends on reading array index locations. That's because you don't want the sprite's x/y position to evaluate to an array index number that's less than or greater than the number of elements in the array. If it does, you might encounter some mysterious "undefined" error messages. These are very hard to track down, especially if they happen infrequently. But that's not the worst that can happen. The worst is that you **won't get any error messages at all**. Instead, you'll just notice all sorts of crazy random bugs with no apparent cause. If that happens, check your sprites' index and position values!

In upcoming examples you'll see how keeping sprites aligned to grid rows and columns makes it easy to implement a maze game with walls.

Collisions with Moving Sprites

What would happen if all the bombs were all moving around? Their map index numbers would change constantly. To help keep track of this, add another new property to your sprites called gid.

playerSprite.**gid**

gid stores the grid index number that references the sprite's image on the tileset. If the a player sprites's tileset image is the fourth on the top row, you could set its gid to 4, like this:

playerSprite.gid = 4;

The makeTileWorld function you learned in the previous chapter added a gid property to all the sprites for you when it created the game world.

If sprites are moving around, use their gid and index properties to update their locations in the map array in real time. Use an updateMap function to help you do this. updateMap takes the original array and a sprite, or an array of sprites, whose locations you want to update. It also needs to know the world's width, height, and widthInTiles. It returns a new array with the new locations of those sprites.

mapArray = updateMap(mapArray, bombSprites, world);

Here's the complete updateMap function that does all the work. (Note that this code makes use of the getIndex function you learned earlier in the chapter).

```
function updateMap(mapArray, spritesToUpdate, world) {

  //First create a map a new array filled with zeros.
  //The new map array will be exactly the same size as the original
  let newMapArray = mapArray.map(gid =>  {
    gid = 0;
    return gid;
  });
```

```
//Is `spriteToUpdate` an array of sprites?
if (spritesToUpdate instanceof Array) {

  //Get the index number of each sprite in the `spritesToUpdate` array
  //and add the sprite's `gid` to the matching index on the map
  spritesToUpdate.forEach(sprite => {

    //Find the new index number
    sprite.index = getIndex(
      sprite.centerX, sprite.centerY,
      world.tilewidth, world.tileheight, world.widthInTiles
    );

    //Add the sprite's `gid` number to the correct
    //index on the map
    newMapArray[sprite.index] = sprite.gid;
  });
}

//Is `spritesToUpdate` just a single sprite?
else {
  let sprite = spritesToUpdate;

  //Find the new index number
  sprite.index = getIndex(
    sprite.centerX, sprite.centerY,
    world.tilewidth, world.tileheight, world.widthInTiles
  );

  //Add the sprite's `gid` number to the correct
  //index on the map
  newMapArray[sprite.index] = sprite.gid;
}

//Return the new map array to replace the previous one
return newMapArray;
}
```

(You'll find the updateMap function in hexi/src/modules/tileUtilities/src/tileUtilities.js.)

updateMap takes an array of sprites, uses their index positions to make a new map, and replaces the previous map with the new one. This is the most reliable way to make sure all the positions are current, and allows for two or more sprites to share a single gid number at the same location. updateMap should be called inside a game loop, after the positions of sprites have been changed, and before you check for collisions.

Now that you know how to update a map in real time, how can you use this information to check for collisions?

Checking Collisions by Comparing Array Locations

If you have lots of moving sprites in a game, you can check for collisions using an array comparison technique. In the first example in this chapter, we checked for a collision between the alien and a bomb like this:

```
if (bombArray[alien.index] === 5) //Collision!
```

This works well for checking a single sprite against a group of sprites. But what if you want to check a group of moving sprites against another group of moving sprites?

The trick is to overlay one map onto another map. If anything in those maps share the same index numbers, you have a collision.

Here's the basic system at work:

First, start with two maps containing different kinds of things. mapOne stores "1"s and mapTwo stores "2"s:

```
mapOne = [0, 0, 1, 0, 1, 0];
mapTwo = [0, 2, 0, 0, 2, 0];
```

What you want to find out is if there are any map locations that are occupied by both a 1 and a 2? Are there? We can clearly see that there are. At index number 4.

But how can we check for this with code? Like this:

```
mapOne.forEach((gid, index) => {
  if (mapTwo[index] === 2 && gid === 1) {
    console.log("Collision at location: " + index);
  }
});
```

This displays:

```
Collision at location: 4
```

If you have lots of sprites with constantly changing positions, this might be the most efficient way to check for collisions.

Let's look at a practical example that demonstrates these new techniques. Run the movingCollision. html file for new a version of the example game with moving bombs. Use the arrow keys to make the alien chase and collect bombs, as shown in Figure 3-6.

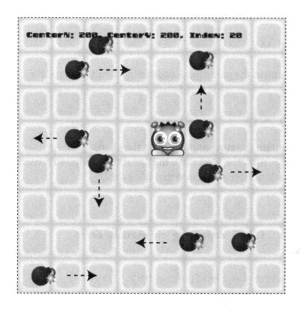

Figure 3-6. *Chase moving bombs around the map*

This new example uses the same three map layers: "backgroundLayer," "bombLayer," and "alienLayer." Figure 3-7 shows the data array for each layer.

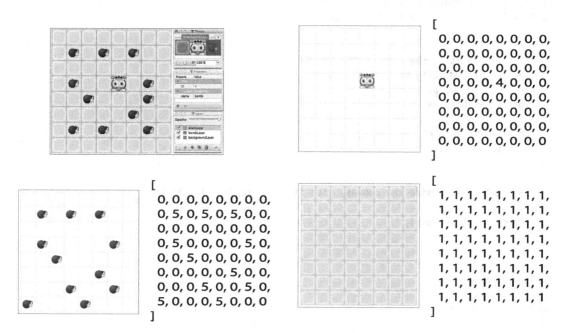

Figure 3-7. *Three map layers in Tiled Editor*

The `setup` function grabs a reference to the alien layer's data array like this:

```
alienMapArray = world.getObject("alienLayer").data;
```

Then, after the alien's position is changed each frame in the game loop, `updateMap` is called to update the alien's position in the array.

```
alienMapArray = updateMap(alienMapArray, alien, world);
```

This means that the `alienMapArray` will always contain the current position of the alien.

The bomb's positions are updated in a `forEach` loop. After the loop runs, the `updateMap` function is used to update the `bombMapArray` with each bomb's new location. Here's the code that does this:

```
bombSprites.forEach(bomb => {

//`atXEdge` and `atYEdge` will return `true` or `false` depending on whether or
//not the sprite is at the edges of the canvas
let atXEdge = (sprite, container) => {
  return (sprite.x === 0 || sprite.x + sprite.width === container.width)
}
let atYEdge = (sprite, container) => {
  return (sprite.y === 0 || sprite.y + sprite.width === container.height)
}

//Change the bomb's direction if it's at a map grid column or row
if (Math.floor(bomb.x) % world.tilewidth === 0
&& Math.floor(bomb.y) % world.tileheight === 0)
{

  //If the bomb is at the edge of the canvas,
  //reverse its velocity to keep it inside
  if (atXEdge(bomb, g.canvas)) {
    bomb.vx = -bomb.vx;
  }
  else if (atYEdge(bomb, g.canvas)) {
    bomb.vy = -bomb.vy;
  }

  //If the bomb is inside the canvas, give it a new random direction
  else {
    changeDirection(bomb);
  }
}

//Move the bomb
bomb.x += bomb.vx;
bomb.y += bomb.vy;
});
```

`bombMapArray` will now contain a current record of the position of the bombs for this frame. You'll notice in the code above that a function called `changeDirection` is called whenever a bomb is centered over a grid cell – let's find out how that works next.

Giving the Bombs a Random Direction

The bombs only change direction if they're aligned to a grid row or column. And, the bombs can't change direction if they're at the edges of the canvas, which prevents them from generating invalid array index numbers. Here's the changeDirection function, which is called whenever these conditions are met.

```
//Change direction helper function
function changeDirection(sprite) {
  let up = 1,
    down = 2,
    left = 3,
    right = 4,
    direction = g.randomInt(1, 4);

  switch (direction) {
    case right:
      sprite.vx = 2;
      sprite.vy = 0;
      break;

    case left:
      sprite.vx = -2;
      sprite.vy = 0;
      break;

    case up:
      sprite.vx = 0;
      sprite.vy = -2;
      break;

    case down:
      sprite.vx = 0;
      sprite.vy = 2;
      break;
  }
}
```

This is just a very simple switch statement that changes the velocity of the sprite to match its randomly assigned direction.

Collision Detection

If you take a snapshot of the alienMapArray or bombMapArray at any time, you'll see that their contents match the locations of the sprites on the canvas, as shown in Figure 3-8.

```
[                                              [
  0, 0, 0, 0, 0, 0, 0, 0,                        0, 0, 0, 0, 0, 0, 0, 0,
  0, 0, 0, 0, 0, 0, 0, 0,                        0, 0, 5, 0, 0, 0, 5, 0,
  0, 0, 0, 0, 0, 0, 0, 0,                        0, 5, 5, 0, 0, 5, 0, 0,
  0, 0, 0, 0, 0, 0, 0, 0,                        0, 0, 0, 0, 0, 0, 0, 0,
  0, 0, 0, 0, 0, 0, 0, 0,                        0, 0, 0, 5, 0, 5, 0, 0,
  0, 0, 0, 0, 0, 0, 0, 0,                        0, 0, 0, 0, 0, 0, 0, 0,
  0, 4, 0, 0, 0, 0, 0, 0,                        0, 0, 0, 0, 5, 0, 0, 0,
  0, 0, 0, 0, 0, 0, 0, 0                         0, 0, 0, 5, 0, 0, 0, 0
]                                              ]
```

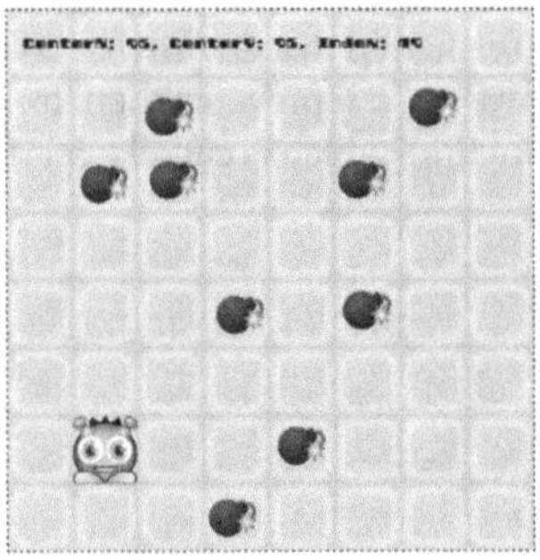

Figure 3-8. Update the sprite's map locations in real time

The collisions are detected by comparing these two arrays. The code loops through the bombMapArray and checks whether the gid of each index position is "5." If it is, and the alienMapArray has a "4" at the same index number, then there's a collision. The code then filters out any bomb sprites at that location. (There might be more than one bomb at that same location). When it finds a match, the bomb is cleared from the map and the sprite is removed.

```
bombMapArray.forEach((gid, index) => {

  //Does the alien have the same index number as a bomb?
  if (alienMapArray[index] === 4 && gid === 5) {

    //Yes, so filter out any bomb sprites at this location
    //(there might be more than one)
    bombSprites = bombSprites.filter(bomb => {
      if (bomb.index === index) {

        //Remove the bomb gid number from the array
        bombMapArray[bomb.index] = 0;

        //Remove the bomb from the `bombLayer` group
        g.remove(bomb);
        return false;
      } else {
        return true;
      }
    });
  }
});
```

So far all these examples have shown you how to check for collisions by using the center points of sprites. But for many games you'll need a little more precision. Let's find out how to make our collision detection a little more accurate.

Using Corner Points

A limitation in our collision system so far is that we're only using the sprite's center x/y point to figure out its map array location.

```
sprite.index = getIndex
  sprite.centerX, sprite.centerY,
  world.tilewidth, world.tileheight, world.widthInTiles
);
```

That means that even if the sprite is part way into the next cell, getIndex won't detect that its location has changed. It will only detect a change if the sprite's center point crosses the cell boundary. You can see in Figure 8-9 that even though the alien is touching the bomb, a collision isn't detected until the center of the alien enters the bomb's cell. See Figure 3-9.

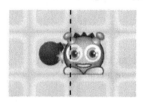 

Figure 3-9. *The sprite's center point is used to figure out its map location*

This might not be a problem, and in fact the effect seems completely natural in this example. But for many kinds of collisions you'll want to use the exact edges of a sprite as the collision boundary. This is important for collisions with things where there should be no overlap at all, such as with walls, or for things were there should be an immediate reaction, like with fire.

So how can you figure out whether the edge of a sprite is in a new map location? Don't use the center point. Instead, use each of the sprite's 4 corner points. Figure 3-10 shows where these four corner points are.

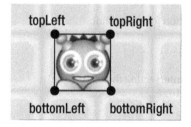

Figure 3-10. *For more precision, check the locations of the sprite's 4 corners*

It's easy to calculate these. Use a getPoints function to calculate and return an object that contains the x/y coordinates of these four points. getPoints takes one argument: the sprite for which you find the corner points. It returns an object with four sub-object properties that tell you the x and y positions of the sprite's corners: topLeft, topRight, bottomLeft, and bottomRight.

```
function getPoints(s) {
  return {
    topLeft: {x: s.x, y: s.y},
    topRight: {x: s.x + s.width - 1, y: s.y},
    bottomLeft: {x: s.x, y: s.y + s.height - 1},
    bottomRight: {x: s.x + s.width - 1, y: s.y + s.height - 1}
  };
}
```

(The bottom and left corner points are 1 pixel less than the sprite's width and height so that the points remain inside the sprite, and not outside it).

■ **Note**   Why use "s" instead of "sprite" in the getCorners function? Although I usually recommend using descriptive variable names, you can make dense and repetitive math calculations more compact and readable by using an obvious shorthand.

Now instead of just checking the sprite's center point to find the map location, check all four corner points. If they have the same index as the gid of the sprite you're interested in, you have a collision.

First, use the above getPoints function to find the sprite's four corner points.

```
sprite.collisionPoints = getPoints(sprite);
```

Create a collisionGid variable that stores the gid of the cell you want to check for a collision with the sprite.

```
let collisionGid = 5;
```

You also need a mapArray that contains sprites that have the above collisionGid.

```
let mapArray = anyMapArray;
```

Then loop through all four points and call a custom checkPoints function for each point.

```
let hit = Object.keys(sprite.collisionPoints).some(checkPoints);
```

The checkPoints function returns true if any of the corner points are intersecting the cells in the mapArray that have the same gid as the collisionGid that we're interested in.

```
function checkPoints(key) {

  //Get a reference to the current point to check.
  //(`topLeft`, `topRight`, `bottomLeft` or `bottomRight` )
  let point = sprite.collisionPoints[key];

  //Find the point's index number in the map array
  let index = getIndex(
    point.x, point.y,
    world.tilewidth, world.tileheight, world.widthInTiles
  );
```

```
//Find out what the gid value is in the map position
//that the point is currently over
let currentGid = mapArray[index];

//If it matches the value of the gid that we're interested, in
//then there's been a collision
if (currentGid === collisionGid) {
  return true;
} else {
  return false;
}
}
```

The above code will return true if *some* of the corners (at least one) are touching the cell you're interested in. That's because we used JavaScript's some array method:

```
var hit = Object.keys(sprite.collisionPoints).some(checkPoints);
```

The loop will quit and the function will return true as soon as it finds the first corner point in the collision. That means that if at the first point, the sprite's topLeft corner gets a hit, the loop will return true right away and not bother checking the other points. This is useful to ensure an immediate reaction to touching something.

But what if you want to detect a collision only if every corner point is touching the cell you're interested in? Use JavaScript's every array method, like this:

```
var hit = Object.keys(sprite.collisionPoints).every(checkPoints);
```

In this case, hit will only become true if every corner point is involved in the collision. This is useful for ensuring that a sprite is completely inside a cell, or covering another sprite. You can use this to very efficiently test whether all four corners of a sprite are on the floor of the maze, so that the sprite doesn't walk through any walls. (You'll see how to do this in the examples ahead).

Now that you know whether or you have a hit, use the index number to find the matching sprite at that same map location. This just a variation on the same code you've seen in previous examples:

```
if (hit) {
  enemySprites.some((enemy) => {
    if (enemy.index === collisionIndex) {

      //This is the sprite you're interested in
    }
  });
}
```

Before we go any further, let's consolidate all this new code.

A Reusable Tile-Based Collision Function

You can see now how useful tile-based collision can be for a wide variety of different game situations. To make our lives a little easier, I've whipped up a general-purpose hitTestTile function so that you can implement tile-based collision with just one line of code. You can drop it into any game with sprites that have the same properties that we've been using in this book. The function checks for a collision between a sprite and a tile gid number on any map array. The function also lets you set the type of collision you want to check for: the center point, some corner points, or every corner point. Here's how to use it:

```
let collisionObject = hitTestTile(sprite, mapArray, collisionGid, worldObject, pointsToCheck);
```

hitTestTile returns a collision object that contains these two properties:

- collision.hit: A Boolean value that will be true if a collision occurred.
- collision.index: A number that tells you the collision's map array location.

You can use these two properties to figure out how to handle the collision.

The fourth argument, worldObject, is an object that defines the tile-based game world. It needs to have these properties:

```
world.tilewidth
world.tileheight
world.widthInTiles
```

(The widthInTiles is a number that represents the number of columns in your tile map).

The makeTiledWorld function that we've been using in the last two chapters automatically returns a world object with these properties for you. But if you are generating your world map from code, without using Tiled Editor, you can still use hitTestTile as long as you pass it your own world object with those same three properties.

The last argument, pointsToCheck, determines which points on the sprite to check for a collision. You can use either of these three string options:

```
"every"
"some"
"center"
```

Here's the complete hitTestTile function. There's no new code here, it's just a reworking of the same techniques we've used in earlier examples.

```
hitTestTile(sprite, mapArray, gidToCheck, world, pointsToCheck) {

  //The `checkPoints` helper function loops through the sprite's corner points to
  //find out if they are inside an array cell that you're interested in.
  //Return `true` if they are
  let checkPoints = key => {

    //Get a reference to the current point to check.
    //(`topLeft`, `topRight`, `bottomLeft` or `bottomRight` )
    let point = sprite.collisionPoints[key];

    //Find the point's index number in the map array
    collision.index = this.getIndex(
      point.x, point.y,
      world.tilewidth, world.tileheight, world.widthInTiles
    );
```

```
    //Find out what the gid value is in the map position
    //that the point is currently over
    collision.gid = mapArray[collision.index];

    //If it matches the value of the gid that we're interested, in
    //then there's been a collision
    if (collision.gid === gidToCheck) {
      return true;
    } else {
      return false;
    }
  };

  //Assign "some" as the default value for `pointsToCheck`
  pointsToCheck = pointsToCheck || "some";

  //The collision object that will be returned by this function
  let collision = {};

  //Which points do you want to check?
  //"every", "some" or "center"?
  switch (pointsToCheck) {
    case "center":

      //`hit` will be true only if the center point is touching
      let point = {
        center: {
          x: sprite.centerX,
          y: sprite.centerY
        }
      };
      sprite.collisionPoints = point;
      collision.hit = Object.keys(sprite.collisionPoints).some(checkPoints);
      break;

    case "every":

      //`hit` will be true if every point is touching
      sprite.collisionPoints = this.getPoints(sprite);
      collision.hit = Object.keys(sprite.collisionPoints).every(checkPoints);
      break;

    case "some":

      //`hit` will be true only if some points are touching
      sprite.collisionPoints = this.getPoints(sprite);
      collision.hit = Object.keys(sprite.collisionPoints).some(checkPoints);
      break;
  }
```

```
//Return the collision object.
//`collision.hit` will be true if a collision is detected.
//`collision.index` tells you the map array index number where the
//collision occured
return collision;
}
```

(You'll find the working version of this function in the chapter's source files at hexi/src/modules/tileUtilities/src).

Run the usingCornerPoints.html example to a see practical example of hitTestTile in action. In this example, the bombs will disappear the very moment any of the alien's corner points enter a cell that contains a bomb. You can see this illustrated in Figure 3-11.

Figure 3-11. *Immediate collision detection by using some of the corner points*

Does that collision reaction appear too immediate? You can achieve a completely different effect by changing "some" to "every":

```
let alienVsBomb = hitTestTile(alien, bombMapArray, 5, world, "every");
```

Now the collision will only be detected when every corner point is inside the bomb's cell. This lets the alien completely envelop the bomb before it disappears. Figure 3-12 illustrates this.

Figure 3-12. *Detect a collision only when every corner point is inside the map cell*

The result is very natural looking, and it's an effect that's difficult to achieve using a geometry-based collision detection system. It also turns out that checking for collisions with every corner point has another important use: you can use it to contain a sprite inside specific map locations. Let's find out how to do that next.

Using Inverse Collision Detection to Check for Obstacles

For maze or RPG games you usually need to know which parts of the map are areas that a character can walk on, and which they can't. For example, a character should be able to walk on grass, but not walls, rocks, or trees. These are known as the walkable and non-walkable areas of a map. Often you'll find that there is only one thing that a character should be allowed to walk on, but many things that it shouldn't be allowed to walk on. So, instead of checking for collision with three things that a character can't walk on (like walls, rocks, and trees) just test for a collision with the one thing that the character can walk on (like grass.) If the character is on the grass, it can walk, but if it's touching anything else, it can't. This is an *inverse* collision strategy. It's inverse because you're finding out whether a sprite is hitting an obstacle by checking whether it's *not hitting* another obstacle. If it's on the grass, you know it's not touching a wall, rock, or tree. Simple! For certain types of collisions this can be very efficient.

How can you find out if a sprite is completely inside a certain map cell? By checking every one of its four corner points. If the sprite's four corners are all at the same location, you know that the sprite is not overlapping any other cell. And, yes, you might not be surprised to learn that you can check for this by using JavaScript's every loop! Let's find out how to do this with the classic example: maze walls.

Run the wallsAndBombs.js file and use the arrow keys to navigate the alien around a maze and pick up the bombs. The alien can move smoothly through the corridors and around corners, but walls block its movement, as shown in Figure 3-13.

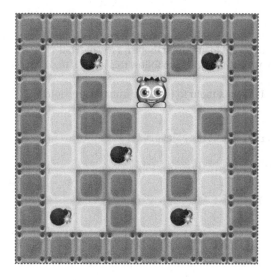

Figure 3-13. Navigate the maze to pick up bombs

Figure 3-14 shows the maze and the wallArray that's used to create it.

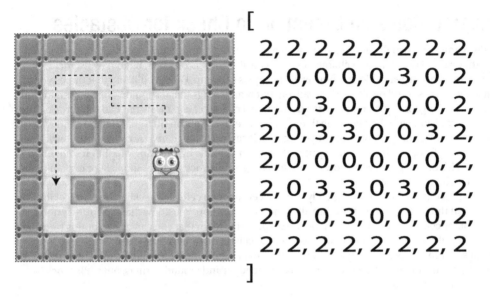

```
[
2, 2, 2, 2, 2, 2, 2, 2,
2, 0, 0, 0, 0, 3, 0, 2,
2, 0, 3, 0, 0, 0, 0, 2,
2, 0, 3, 3, 0, 0, 3, 2,
2, 0, 0, 0, 0, 0, 0, 2,
2, 0, 3, 3, 0, 3, 0, 2,
2, 0, 0, 3, 0, 0, 0, 2,
2, 2, 2, 2, 2, 2, 2, 2
]
```

Figure 3-14. Add walls to create a maze game

You can see that anything with a gid number of 2 or 3 is a wall. But because we're going to do an inverse collision check, we're not interested in those. We're only interested in anything that isn't a wall. That's anything represented by a "0" in the map. So our collision algorithm is going to follow this logic: *If the alien isn't touching a "0" cell, prevent it from moving.*

Here's all the code from the game loop that does this. It's very similar to the code from the previous example, except for a few small details.

```
let alienVsFloor = g.hitTestTile(alien, wallMapArray, 0, world, "every");

if (!alienVsFloor.hit) {

  //Prevent the alien from moving
  alien.x -= alien.vx;
  alien.y -= alien.vy;
  alien.vx = 0;
  alien.vy = 0;
}
```

You can see that `alienVsFloor` only becomes `true` if every corner point is inside a "0" cell. If `alienVsFloor` becomes `false`, we know that the alien is touching something that isn't "0" – and that thing must be a wall.

This example uses the world's simplest collision reaction code. If the alien hits a wall, the alien is prevented from moving by subtracting its velocity from its position, and then setting its velocity to zero.

```
alien.x -= alien.vx;
alien.y -= alien.vy;
alien.vx = 0;
alien.vy = 0;
```

We can get away with such a simple collision reaction system because the alien's movement is aligned to the map's grid rows and columns, and we're not using any physics to change its velocity. Those constraints have removed a whole class of collision problems that we don't have to worry about.

To see how this code is used in context, here's all the code from the game loop that uses hitTestTile to check for a collision between the alien and the floor, and the alien and the bombs.

```
//Check for a collision between the alien and floor
let alienVsFloor = g.hitTestTile(alien, wallMapArray, 0, world, "every");

//Prevent the alien from moving if it's not touching a floor tile
if (!alienVsFloor.hit) {
  alien.x -= alien.vx;
  alien.y -= alien.vy;
  alien.vx = 0;
  alien.vy = 0;
}

//Check for a collision between the alien and the bombs
let alienVsBomb = g.hitTestTile(alien, bombMapArray, 5, world, "every");

//Find out if the alien's position in the bomb array matches a bomb gid number
if (alienVsBomb.hit) {

  //If it does, filter through the bomb sprites and find the one
  //that matches the alien's position
  bombSprites = bombSprites.filter(function(bomb) {

    //Does the bomb sprite have the same index number as the alien?
    if (bomb.index === alienVsBomb.index) {

      //If it does, remove the bomb from the
      //`bombMapArray` by setting its gid to `0`
      bombMapArray[bomb.index] = 0;

      //Remove the bomb sprite from its container group
      g.remove(bomb);

      //Filter the bomb out of the `bombSprites` array
      return false;
    } else {

      //Keep the bomb in the `bombSprites` array if it doesn't match
      return true;
    }
  });
}
```

Now we've got a useful tile-based collision system we can use for all kinds of tile-based games. So let's now find out how we can use all these new skills in the fantasy Role Playing game that we started to build in the previous chapter.

Tile-Based Collision for Role Playing Games

Play through the fantasy.html prototype example from Chapter 1 to re-acquaint yourself with how it behaves. You'll notice that the elf character can collide with two types of things:

- Obstacles that prevent movement: the bottoms of trees, the bottoms of walls, and the bottoms of bushes.

- Items that can be collected: the heart, the skull, and the marmot.

Figure 3-15 illustrates this. The collision mechanics are all based on the tile-based collision system we learned in the previous few sections. But there are a few interesting new details, which far from being edge-cases, are typical of collision problems you'll need to solve for many kinds of games.

Figure 3-15. *Obstacles block movement and items can be collected*

Defining the Collision Area

All the tiles in the game map are comprised of graphics that neatly fill 32 by 32 pixel square tiles. The elf character, however, doesn't follow this pattern. Its sprite size is 64 by 64 pixels, and the actual size of the character illustration is 28 by 52 pixels. Figure 3-16 illustrates this.

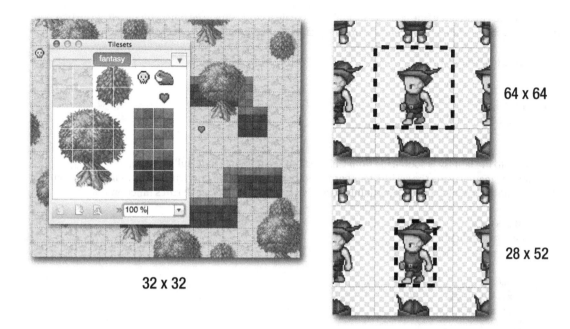

64 x 64

28 x 52

32 x 32

Figure 3-16. *All the sizes are different*

This wasn't an issue in the maze game examples, because the tile sizes, sprite sizes, and maze cell grid sizes were all exactly the same: 64x64 pixels. What do we do now?

Relax! Just create a collision area on the elf. The collision area defines which part of the elf should be sensitive to collisions. In this game, I only want the area of the elf's body below its head to react to collisions. It's a square area of 20 by 20 pixels, that you can see in Figure 3-17. It's offset by the top of the sprite by 44 pixels, and offset on the left by 22 pixels.

Figure 3-17. *The sprite's collision area*

This preserves the shallow 2.5D depth effect because it means the elf's head won't bump into things that are visually above it but on a lower depth layer – like the tops of walls or trees.

To set this up in our game code we just need to create a collisionArea object on the elf sprite that defines this shape. Here's the bit of code from the game's setup function that does this.

```
elf.collisionArea = {
  x: 22,
  y: 44,
  width: 20,
  height: 20
};
```

(Refer to the fantasy.js source file from Chapter 1 to see this code in its full context).

Now, instead of using the sprite's four corner points, do a collision check using the four corner points of this new collisionArea. To implement this, use this new version of the getPoints function.

```
getPoints(s) {
  let ca = s.collisionArea;
  if (ca !== undefined) {
    return {
      topLeft: {
        x: s.x + ca.x,
        y: s.y + ca.y
      },
      topRight: {
        x: s.x + ca.x + ca.width,
        y: s.y + ca.y
      },
      bottomLeft: {
        x: s.x + ca.x,
        y: s.y + ca.y + ca.height
      },
      bottomRight: {
        x: s.x + ca.x + ca.width,
        y: s.y + ca.y + ca.height
      }
    };
  } else {
    return {
      topLeft: {
        x: s.x,
        y: s.y
      },
      topRight: {
        x: s.x + s.width - 1,
        y: s.y
      },
      bottomLeft: {
        x: s.x,
        y: s.y + s.height - 1
      },
```

```
    bottomRight: {
      x: s.x + s.width - 1,
      y: s.y + s.height - 1
    }
  };
  }
}
```

You can now set a custom collision area for any sprites in the game. Now how does the collision system in the fantasy RPG game example work?

Collisions with Obstacles

You'll remember from Chapter 2 that all the tiles that should prevent the elf from moving were created on a map layer called obstacles, shown in Figure 3-18.

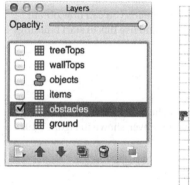
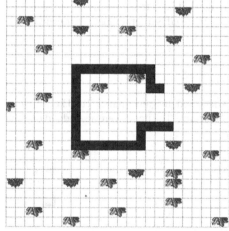

Figure 3-18. *The map's obstacles layer*

This exports as a nice fat array that is full of gid numbers representing the obstacles. But, most importantly, it's also full of zeros. Any "0" in the array means "no obstacle." That means we can use our little inverse collision trick. We can check to see if all four corners of the elf's collision area are touching "0" cells. If any of them aren't "0," we know that the elf has bumped into an obstacle. The code we end up with is almost identical to the code we used to check for maze walls in our earlier maze game examples. Here's the code from the game loop that checks whether the elf is touching an obstacle. If it is, the code prevents the elf from moving.

```
let obstaclesMapArray = world.getObject("obstacles").data;
let elfVsGround = g.hitTestTile(elf, obstaclesMapArray, 0, world, "every");

if (!elfVsGround.hit) {

  //Prevent the elf from moving
  elf.x -= elf.vx;
  elf.y -= elf.vy;
  elf.vx = 0;
  elf.vy = 0;
}
```

What if you want to find out which type of obstacle the elf has bumped into? You can use the `collision.index` property to look up its gid number in the map array. Here's how you could find a gid number from the `obstacleMapArray`:

```
obstaclesMapArray[elfVsGround.index]
```

If the elf bumped into the right side of a tree, this would give you 33. This means you can now obtain detailed information about how of the elf is interacting with the environment, and use this to start building some sophisticated game logic.

Collisions with Items

You'll remember that when we designed the game map in Tiled Editor, we gave the item tiles these name properties: "skull", "heart", and "marmot." The items were also added on their own layer, shown in Figure 3-19.

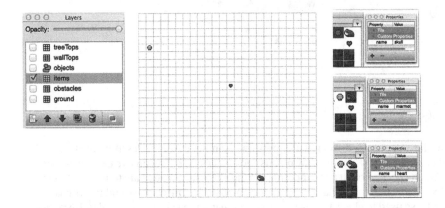

Figure 3-19. *The item tiles are on their own layer and have name properties*

We can use these custom name properties in our game code to tell us which items the elf is touching. Let's find out how.

First, we need to get a reference to the items layer.

```
itemsLayer = world.getObject("items");
```

Remember that itemsLayer is a sprite container. It contains all the sprites on that layer; there will only be three: the heart, skull, and marmot. You can access those sprites in the layer's children array. So the next step to get a reference to the itemsLayer.children.

```
items = itemsLayer.children;
```

We now have an array called items that contains the three item sprites.

■ **Note** Alternatively, you might want to *clone* the array instead of making a direct reference pointer to the original. You can clone the array like this:

```
items = itemsLayer.children.slice(0);
```

The advantage to cloning the array is that if you make changes to the items array, the orginal itemsLayer.children array will remain unmodified. This could be very useful if you need to reset the game to its original state.

How does the collision between the elf and items work? No surprises! It's exactly the same as the collision between the bombs and alien in the earlier examples from this chapter. The only addition is that, when a collision happens, a message is displayed on screen for three seconds that give you the name of the item the elf has collected.

```
let itemsMapArray = world.getObject("items").data;
let elfVsItems = g.hitTestTile(elf, itemsMapArray, 0, world, "some");

if (!elfVsItems.hit) {
items = items.filter(item => {

  //Does the current item match the elf's position?
  if (item.index === elfVsItems.index) {

    //Display the message
    message.visible = true;
    message.content = "You found a " + item.name;

    //Make the message disappear after 3 seconds
    g.wait(3000, function() {
      message.visible = false;
    });

    //Remove the item
    itemsMapArray[item.index] = 0;
    g.remove(item);
    return false;
  } else {
    return true;
  }
  });
}
```

Figure 3-20 illustrates the message that will appear onscreen when an item is collected.

Figure 3-20. *Display the item's name property*

Tile-based collision: solved!

Summary

Tile-based collision is one of the most useful game design techniques you can learn. The simple systems that we used in this chapter can be used as the basis for most, or all, of the collision you'll need to do in 2D action games. You now how to find an object's location on world map, check it for collisions with other other objects, react to those collisions, and update the game world. You can use the general purpose `hitTestTile` function, along with `getIndex` and `getPoints` for handling collisions for any 2D videogame of any genre.

But would it surprise you if you I told you, yet again, that "We're not done yet!"? Now that you understand how to make an interactive tile-based game world, a whole new universe of game design techniques has opened up to you. Over the next few chapters we're going to feast on all these new techniques: influence maps, broadphase collision, pathfinding, procedural level generation and, in the next chapter, isometric maps. I hope you're hungry!

CHAPTER 4

Isometric Maps

Now that you know the basics of making tile-based games, let's add a cool new feature: **isometric projection**. Isometric projection is a shallow 3D effect in which the game world appears to be rotated by 45 degrees and viewed from above at a 30 degree angle. Figure 4-1 shows a typical isometric map layout.

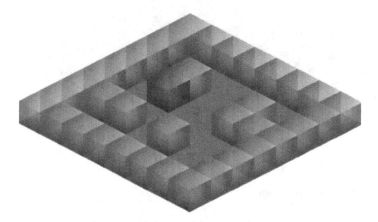

Figure 4-1. *Isometric projection is a fixed-perspective 3D effect*

Instead of squares, your map is made up of shapes that represent cubes, as seen edge-on at an angle. It looks 3D, but there are two big differences between isometric 3D and true 3D:

- Isometric 3D has a permanently fixed perspective.

- Isometric 3D doesn't have a horizon line, so the game world can appear to extend endlessly beyond the edges of the world.

Isometric maps are standard for many genres of games, such as strategy and map-based adventure and role playing games. Their strength is that, like 2D maps, they give the player a consistent bird's-eye view of the game world, so it's easy to plot and plan your next move. But the 3D perspective can give you a greater sensation of spatial immersion than an ordinary 2D map can generally provide.

In this chapter you'll learn all the basics of how to make an isometric game map, including how to do the following:

- Move a game character around an isometric world.

- Accurately depth sort sprites.

© Rex van der Spuy 2017
R. van der Spuy, *The Advanced Game Developer's Toolkit*, DOI 10.1007/978-1-4842-1097-0_4

- Do collision detection between isometric sprites.

- Use a pointer to select isometric sprites, and match their onscreen locations to their map array index positions.

- How to set up and render an isometric game world using Tiled Editor.

Let's find out how!

Isometric Basics

You might be surprised to learn that the only new thing you need to know to make an isometric game world is a little bit of easy math. Take a look at Figure 4-2, which renders the same game map in two ways.

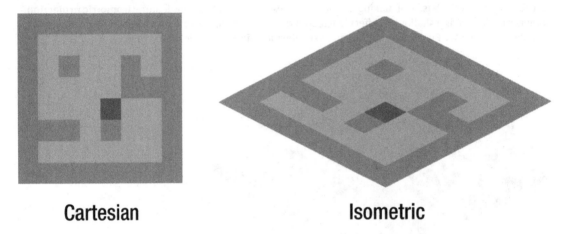

Figure 4-2. *Cartsian vs. Isometric rendering of the same map*

Both maps were created using identical map array data. The example on the left renders the map using **Cartesian coordinates**. These are what we know as ordinary x and y coordinates that align to the axis planes at right angles. The example on the right renders the map using **isometric coordinates**. There's only one difference between the two maps: the tiles in the isometric map are just stretched and rotated by 45 degrees. It's the same map, just seen through a different lens. What that means is that you can turn any ordinary Cartesian tile map into an isometric tile map just by applying a simple mathematical conversion.

Here's pretty much the only math you need to know to convert x and y points between a flat Cartesian map and a 3D isometric map. To convert Cartesian x and y points to isometric points, use this formula:

```
isoX = cartX - cartY;
isoY = (cartX + cartY) / 2;
```

To convert isometric points to Cartesian, use this formula:

```
cartX = (2 * isoY + isoX) / 2;
cartY = (2 * isoY - isoX) / 2;
```

That's all! The rest of the code you'll be learning in this chapter is essentially just giving you an easy way to convert between these two coordinate systems, using these formulas.

Making a Cartesian Tile Map

Before we begin our adventure into the world of isometric projection, let's get back to basics for a moment and find out how to make the Cartesian tile map in Figure 4-2. This is also a good model of a bare-bones tile map rendering system that you can scale into something more full-featured if you later need to. Here's the code from the setup function in the cartesian.js file in this book's source code that produces the map – the comments describe step by step how the code works.

```
//Create the `world` container that defines our isometric
//tile-based world
let world = g.group();

//Set the Cartesian dimensions of each tile, in pixels
world.cartTilewidth = 32;
world.cartTileheight = 32;

//Define the width and height of the world, in tiles
world.widthInTiles = 8;
world.heightInTiles = 8;

//Create the world layers
world.layers = [

  //The environment layer. `2` represents the walls,
  //`1` represents the floors
  [
    2, 2, 2, 2, 2, 2, 2, 2,
    2, 1, 1, 1, 1, 1, 1, 2,
    2, 1, 2, 1, 1, 2, 1, 2,
    2, 1, 1, 1, 1, 2, 2, 2,
    2, 1, 1, 1, 1, 1, 1, 2,
    2, 2, 2, 1, 2, 1, 1, 2,
    2, 1, 1, 1, 1, 1, 1, 2,
    2, 2, 2, 2, 2, 2, 2, 2
  ],

  //The character layer. `3` represents the game character
  //`0` represents an empty cell which won't contain any
  //sprites
  [
    0, 0, 0, 0, 0, 0, 0, 0,
    0, 0, 0, 0, 0, 0, 0, 0,
    0, 0, 0, 0, 0, 0, 0, 0,
    0, 0, 0, 0, 0, 0, 0, 0,
    0, 0, 0, 0, 3, 0, 0, 0,
    0, 0, 0, 0, 0, 0, 0, 0,
    0, 0, 0, 0, 0, 0, 0, 0,
    0, 0, 0, 0, 0, 0, 0, 0
  ]
];
```

```
//Build the game world by looping through each
//of the layers arrays one after the other
world.layers.forEach(layer => {

  //Loop through each array element
  layer.forEach((gid, index) => {

    //If the cell isn't empty (0) then create a sprite
    if (gid !== 0) {

      //Find the column and row that the sprite is on and also
      //its x and y pixel values that match column and row position
      let column, row, x, y;
      column = index % world.widthInTiles;
      row = Math.floor(index / world.widthInTiles);
      x = column * world.cartTilewidth;
      y = row * world.cartTileheight;

      //Next, create a different sprite based on what its
      //`gid` number is
      let sprite;
      switch (gid) {

        //The floor
        case 1:
          sprite = g.rectangle(world.cartTilewidth, world.cartTileheight, 0xCCCCFF);
          break;

        //The walls
        case 2:
          sprite = g.rectangle(world.cartTilewidth, world.cartTileheight, 0x99CC00);
          break;

        //The character
        case 3:
          sprite = g.rectangle(world.cartTilewidth, world.cartTileheight, 0xFF0000);
      }

      //Position the sprite using the calculated `x` and `y` values
      //that match its column and row in the tile map
      sprite.x = x;
      sprite.y = y;

      //Add the sprite to the `world` container
      world.addChild(sprite);
    }
  });
});
```

■ **Note**   The `rectangle` function in the code above just displays a rectangle of a given width, height, and color.

Now let's find out how to display this same map in an isometric view.

Making an Isometric Tile Map

There are two things we need to add to create our new isometric map. The first is an isometric square sprite that we can use to display each tile. The second is a way to convert Cartesian coordinates (normal x and y coordinates) to isometric coordinates.

Isometric Sprites

An isometric tile sprite is just a square that's been rotated by 45 degrees and squashed to half its height, as shown in Figure 4-3.

Figure 4-3. *Use diamond shaped tiles as the basis for plotting isometric maps*

Here's a function called `isoRectangle` that creates just such a sprite. It's drawn using the PixiJS rendering system, but you can achieve the same effect with any graphics library that lets you draw shapes, including the Canvas API.

```
function isoRectangle(width, height, fillStyle) {

  //Figure out the `halfHeight` value
  let halfHeight = height / 2;

  //Draw the flattened and rotated square (diamond shape)
  let rectangle = new PIXI.Graphics();
  rectangle.beginFill(fillStyle);
  rectangle.moveTo(0, 0);
  rectangle.lineTo(width, halfHeight);
  rectangle.lineTo(0, height);
  rectangle.lineTo(-width, halfHeight);
  rectangle.lineTo(0, 0);
  rectangle.endFill();

  //Generate a texture from the rectangle
  let texture = rectangle.generateTexture();

  //Use the texture to create a sprite
  let sprite = new PIXI.Sprite(texture);

  //Return the sprite to the main program
  return sprite;
}
```

Now that we have a way to generate isometric sprites, we need some way to convert Cartesian x and y coordinates to isometric coordinates.

Figuring Out the Isometric Coordinates

Do you remember the simple conversion formula I showed you at the beginning of this chapter to convert Cartesian x and y points to isometric points?

```
isoX = cartX - cartY;
isoY = (cartX + cartY) / 2;
```

Here's how we can use this formula to add isoX and isoY properties to the sprite object that the isoRectangle function creates.

```
sprite.isoX = sprite.x - sprite.y;
sprite.isoY = (sprite.x + sprite.y) / 2;
```

But to make things easier for us, let's create a function that adds these new isoX and isoY properties to *any* sprite. And, while we're at it, let's also capture the sprites' Cartesian coordinates and dimensions as cartX, cartY, cartWidth, and cartHeight – just in case we need to access them at some later point (spoiler: we will!). Here's the addIsoProperties function that does this.

```
function addIsoProperties(sprite, x, y, width, height){

  //Cartisian (flat 2D) properties
  sprite.cartX = x;
  sprite.cartY = y;
  sprite.cartWidth = width;
  sprite.cartHeight = height;

  //Add a getter/setter for the isometric properties
  Object.defineProperties(sprite, {
    isoX: {
      get() {
        return this.cartX - this.cartY;
      },
      enumerable: true,
      configurable: true
    },
    isoY: {
      get() {
        return (this.cartX + this.cartY) / 2;
      },
      enumerable: true,
      configurable: true
    },
  });
}
```

Just supply this function with any sprite that has ordinary x, y, width, and height properties and it will add the isoX, isoY, and additional Cartesian properties for you.

The rest is now easy! Let's find out just how easy by rendering our original Cartesian tile map from the first example as a new isometric map. Here's the code from the setup function in the isometric.js file. You'll notice that it's the same as the first example, except for the addition of the isoRectangle and addIsoProperties functions that you've just learned.

```
//Create the `world` container that defines our isometric tile-based world
world = g.group();

//Define the size of each tile and the size of the tile map
world.cartTilewidth = 32;
world.cartTileheight = 32;
world.widthInTiles = 8;
world.heightInTiles = 8;

//Create the world layers
world.layers = [

  //The environment layer. `2` represents the walls,
  //`1` represents the floors
  [
    2, 2, 2, 2, 2, 2, 2, 2,
    2, 1, 1, 1, 1, 1, 1, 2,
    2, 1, 2, 1, 1, 2, 1, 2,
    2, 1, 1, 1, 1, 2, 2, 2,
    2, 1, 1, 1, 1, 1, 1, 2,
    2, 2, 2, 1, 2, 1, 1, 2,
    2, 1, 1, 1, 1, 1, 1, 2,
    2, 2, 2, 2, 2, 2, 2, 2
  ],

  //The character layer. `3` represents the game character
  //`0` represents an empty cell which won't contain any
  //sprites
  [
    0, 0, 0, 0, 0, 0, 0, 0,
    0, 0, 0, 0, 0, 0, 0, 0,
    0, 0, 0, 0, 0, 0, 0, 0,
    0, 0, 0, 0, 0, 0, 0, 0,
    0, 0, 0, 0, 3, 0, 0, 0,
    0, 0, 0, 0, 0, 0, 0, 0,
    0, 0, 0, 0, 0, 0, 0, 0,
    0, 0, 0, 0, 0, 0, 0, 0
  ]
];
```

```
//Build the game world by looping through each of the arrays
world.layers.forEach(layer => {

  //Loop through each array element
  layer.forEach((gid, index) => {

    //If the cell isn't empty (0) then create a sprite
    if (gid !== 0) {

      //Find the column and row that the sprite is on and also
      //its x and y pixel values.
      let column, row, x, y;
      column = index % world.widthInTiles;
      row = Math.floor(index / world.widthInTiles);
      x = column * world.cartTilewidth;
      y = row * world.cartTileheight;

      //Next, create a different sprite based on what its `gid` number is
      let sprite;
      switch (gid) {

        //The floor
        case 1:

          //Create a sprite using an isometric rectangle
          sprite = isoRectangle(world.cartTilewidth, world.cartTileheight, 0xCCCCFF);
          break;

        //The walls
        case 2:
          sprite = isoRectangle(world.cartTilewidth, world.cartTileheight, 0x99CC00);
          break;

        //The character
        case 3:
          sprite = isoRectangle(world.cartTilewidth, world.cartTileheight, 0xFF0000);
      }

      //Add these properties to the sprite
      addIsoProperties(sprite, x, y, world.cartTilewidth, world.cartTileheight);

      //Set the sprite's `x` and `y` pixel position based on its
      //isometric coordinates
      sprite.x = sprite.isoX;
      sprite.y = sprite.isoY;

      //Add the sprite to the `world` container
      world.addChild(sprite);
    }
  });
});
```

//Position the world inside the canvas
```
let canvasOffset = (g.canvas.width / 2) - world.cartTilewidth;
world.x += canvasOffset;
```

The last two lines center the isometric world in the canvas.

This should prove to you that any ordinary, square tile map can be re-rendered as an isometric world without changing any of the underlying tile-based logic.

Working with Isometric Properties

Let's now take our new skills one step further and find out how to convert from map array index numbers to isometric coordinates - and back again. Run the pointer.html file in the chapter's source files and move the mouse pointer around the isometric map. You'll notice that the text display tells you the row and column of the map that the pointer is over, its matching array index number, and also the corresponding Cartesian x and y positions, as shown in Figure 4-4.

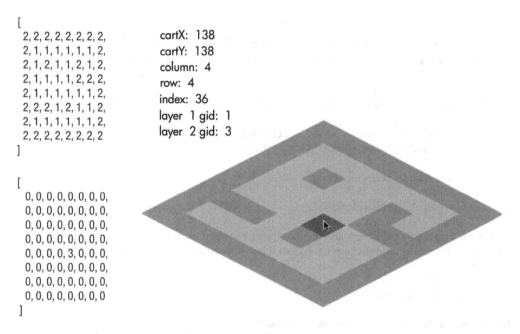

Figure 4-4. *Correlate map array index positions and Cartesian coordinates with isometric locations*

For example, move the pointer onto the red square, and you'll see displayed the gid numbers of both map layers at that location. You'll also see displayed the row and column number that match the tile's location. And, the display also tells you what the Cartesian x and y location of the mouse pointer would be at that position if this were an ordinary 2D map. Useful stuff!

This is essentially your little "Hello World" for working with isometric maps. If you're comfortable doing these kinds of conversions, the more advanced features like character movement and collision will fall neatly into place.

There's nothing new going on here, except that we're using the x and y coordinates of a mouse and a pointer object to help us obtain these values. To convert from isometric coordinates to Cartesian coordinates, the code is just using the same formula I showed you at the beginning of this chapter:

```
cartX = (2 * isoY + isoX) / 2;
cartY = (2 * isoY - isoX) / 2;
```

The only additional refinement we need to make is to compensate for any possible x/y offset of the isometric map in the canvas display area. Here's the code that will do all this.

```
pointer.cartX =
  (((2 * pointer.y + pointer.x) - (2 * world.y + world.x)) / 2)
  - (world.cartTilewidth / 2);

pointer.cartY =
  (((2 * pointer.y - pointer.x) - (2 * world.y - world.x)) / 2)
  + (world.cartTileheight / 2);
```

■ **Note** Any scene graph or game engine that you might be using will have some kind of `pointer` object that will give you these x and y values. Just identify it in the technology you're using and apply this code to it.

With those values in our pocket, we can now easily calculate the tile's row and column location.

```
column = Math.floor(pointer.cartX / world.cartTilewidth);
row = Math.floor(this.cartY / world.cartTileheight);
```

And finally, the map array index number:

```
index = column + (row * world.widthInTiles);
```

To make our lives a little easier, let's add these properties to the pointer object using a function called `makeIsoPointer`. This will let us grab these value from the pointer whenever we need them.

```
function makeIsoPointer(pointer, world) {
  Object.defineProperties(pointer, {

    //The isometric's world's Cartesian coordinates
    cartX: {
      get() {
        let x =
          (((2 * this.y + this.x) - (2 * world.y + world.x)) / 2)
          - (world.cartTilewidth / 2);

        return x;
      },
      enumerable: true,
      configurable: true
    },
```

```
      cartY: {
        get() {
          let y =
            (((2 * this.y - this.x) - (2 * world.y - world.x)) / 2)
            + (world.cartTileheight / 2);

          return y
        },
        enumerable: true,
        configurable: true
      },

      //The tile's column and row in the array
      column: {
        get() {
          return Math.floor(this.cartX / world.cartTilewidth);
        },
        enumerable: true,
        configurable: true
      },
      row: {
        get() {
          return Math.floor(this.cartY / world.cartTileheight);
        },
        enumerable: true,
        configurable: true
      },

      //The tile's index number in the array
      index: {
        get() {
          let index = {};

          //Convert pixel coordinates to map index coordinates
          index.x = Math.floor(this.cartX / world.cartTilewidth);
          index.y = Math.floor(this.cartY / world.cartTileheight);

          //Return the index number
          return index.x + (index.y * world.widthInTiles);
        },
        enumerable: true,
        configurable: true
      },
    });
}
```

You can now add these properties to your pointer like this:

```
makeIsoPointer(g.pointer, world);
```

And you can display them in a text field like this:

```
message.content = `
  cartX: ${Math.floor(g.pointer.cartX)}
  cartY: ${Math.floor(g.pointer.cartY)}
  column: ${g.pointer.column}
  row: ${g.pointer.row}
  index: ${g.pointer.index}
  layer 1 gid: ${world.layers[0][Math.floor(g.pointer.index)]}
  layer 2 gid: ${world.layers[1][Math.floor(g.pointer.index)]}
`;
```

This is the only new code in the pointer.js file in this chapter's source code that produces the output in Figure 4-4 – the rest of the code is the same as our earlier examples.

All of our core skills for working with isometric maps are now in place, so let's see how we can start using them to begin making games.

Moving Around an Isometric World

Let's next find out how to move a game character around this isometric map. Run the movement.html file in the chapter's source files, and use the keyboard arrow keys to move the red square around the maze, as shown in Figure 4-5. A text field displays the map array index number that the red square is currently occupying.

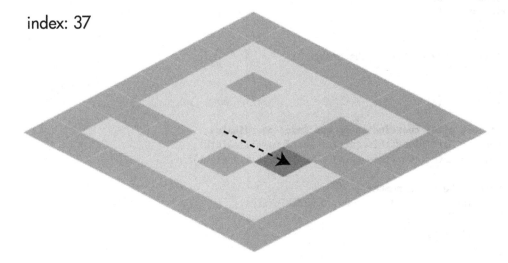

Figure 4-5. *Use the arrow keys to move the red square*

Don't panic - you already know how to do this! All the code is doing is fusing the tile-based map movement techniques you learned in the previous chapter with our new isometric skills. To prove it to, you, let's take a tour of the new code that has been added to our existing code base.

First, you need to define what the "player" character is. In this example, it's the red square. So let's reference it as the player object in the switch statement that plots the tile map.

```
case 3:
  sprite = isoRectangle(world.cartTilewidth, world.cartTileheight, 0xFF0000);
  player = sprite;
```

In the setup function we also need to define keyboard arrow keys and the player object's direction property so that we can move it around the map. Let's add the code to do this, which is identical to code we used to accomplish the same thing in the previous chapter.

```
//Create the keyboard objects
leftArrow = g.keyboard(37);
upArrow = g.keyboard(38);
rightArrow = g.keyboard(39);
downArrow = g.keyboard(40);

//Assign the key `press` actions
player.direction = "none";
leftArrow.press = () => player.direction = "left";
upArrow.press = () => player.direction = "up";
rightArrow.press = () => player.direction = "right";
downArrow.press = () => player.direction = "down";
leftArrow.release = () => player.direction = "none";
upArrow.release = () => player.direction = "none";
rightArrow.release = () => player.direction = "none";
downArrow.release = () => player.direction = "none";
```

The next step is to add code to the game loop that uses the keyboard input to move the player. This is essentially the same code we used to move a sprite on a 2D map, with one important change. Instead of working directly with the sprite's x and y screen position values, the code works with the sprite's cartX and cartY properties. The sprite's position, velocity, and screen boundaries are all updated using cartX and cartY. Only in the final step are the new, calculated isoX and isoY properties used to set the sprite's screen position.

Why? Because doing all your logic and positioning calculations with cartX and cartY means you can write code that is *identical* to the code you would write for an ordinary 2D tile-based map. That means there's nothing new to learn! Here's the code from the game loop that does all this and, as a bonus, tells you tells you which map array index position the sprite is occupying.

```
//Change the player character's velocity if it's centered over a grid cell
if (Math.floor(player.cartX) % world.cartTilewidth === 0
&& Math.floor(player.cartY) % world.cartTileheight === 0) {
  switch (player.direction) {
    case "up":
      player.vy = -2;
      player.vx = 0;
      break;
    case "down":
      player.vy = 2;
      player.vx = 0;
      break;
```

```
      case "left":
        player.vx = -2;
        player.vy = 0;
        break;
      case "right":
        player.vx = 2;
        player.vy = 0;
        break;
      case "none":
        player.vx = 0;
        player.vy = 0;
        break;
    }
}

//Update the player's Cartesian position based on its velocity
player.cartY += player.vy;
player.cartX += player.vx;

//Add world boundaries
let top = 0,
    bottom = (world.heightInTiles * world.cartTileheight),
    left = 0,
    right = (world.widthInTiles * world.cartTilewidth);

//Prevent the player from crossing any of the world boundaries
//Top
if (player.cartY < 0) {
  player.cartY = top;
}

//Bottom
if (player.cartY + player.cartHeight > bottom) {
  player.cartY = bottom - player.cartHeight;
}

//Left
if (player.cartX < left) {
  player.cartX = left;
}

//Right
if (player.cartX + player.cartWidth > right) {
  player.cartX = right - player.cartWidth;
}

//Position the sprite's sceen `x` and `y` position
//using its isometric coordinates
player.x = player.isoX;
player.y = player.isoY;
```

```
//Get the player's index position in the map array
player.index = g.getIndex(
  player.cartX, player.cartY,
  world.cartTilewidth, world.cartTileheight, world.widthInTiles
);
```

```
//Display the player's x, y and index values
message.content = `index: ${player.index}`;
```

Now that we can move a sprite around the game world, the next step is to add collision detection.

Isometric Collision Detection

To make tile-based collision detection work in an isometric world, we need make a few modifications to the getPoints function you learned in the previous chapter. Instead of using the sprite's ordinary x, y, width, and height screen values, we need to use its cartX, cartY, cartWidth, and cartHeight values. Here' a new function called getIsoPoints that implements this.

```
function getIsoPoints(s) {
  let ca = s.collisionArea;
  if (ca !== undefined) {
    return {
      topLeft: {
        x: s.cartX + ca.x,
        y: s.cartY + ca.y
      },
      topRight: {
        x: s.cartX + ca.x + ca.width,
        y: s.cartY + ca.y
      },
      bottomLeft: {
        x: s.cartX + ca.x,
        y: s.cartY + ca.y + ca.height
      },
      bottomRight: {
        x: s.cartX + ca.x + ca.width,
        y: s.cartY + ca.y + ca.height
      }
    };
  }
  else {
    return {
      topLeft: {
        x: s.cartX,
        y: s.cartY
      },
      topRight: {
        x: s.cartX + s.cartWidth - 1,
        y: s.cartY
      },
```

```
        bottomLeft: {
          x: s.cartX,
          y: s.cartY + s.cartHeight - 1
        },
        bottomRight: {
          x: s.cartX + s.cartWidth - 1,
          y: s.cartY + s.cartHeight - 1
        }
      };
    }
  }
}
```

(Remember, ca refers to the sprite's collision area, which you learned about in Chapter 3.)

Now we need to replace the old getPoints with getIsoPoints in the hitTestTile function. We also need to use the sprite's cartX and cartY values to calculate its center point. Let's a use a new version of hitTestTile called hitTestIsoTile that implements this. Here's an abridged version of hitTestIsoTile with the new updated code highlighted.

```
function hitTestIsoTile(sprite, mapArray, gidToCheck, world, pointsToCheck) {

  //...

  switch (pointsToCheck) {

    case "center":
      let point = {
        center: {
          x: s.cartX + ca.x + (ca.width / 2),
          y: s.cartY + ca.y + (ca.height / 2)
        }
      };
      sprite.collisionPoints = point;
      collision.hit = Object.keys(sprite.collisionPoints).some(checkPoints);
      break;

    case "every":
      sprite.collisionPoints = getIsoPoints(sprite);
      collision.hit = Object.keys(sprite.collisionPoints).every(checkPoints);
      break;

    case "some":
      sprite.collisionPoints = getIsoPoints(sprite);
      collision.hit = Object.keys(sprite.collisionPoints).some(checkPoints);
      break;
  }

  //...

}
```

These are the only changes that need to be made by our old `hitTestTile` function. You'll find the complete `hitTestIsoTile` function in the chapter's source files.

We can now use `hitTestIsoTile` in the game loop to check for a collision like this:

```
//Get a reference to the wall map array
wallMapArray = world.layers[0];

//Use `hitTestIsoTile` to check for a collision
let playerVsGround = hitTestIsoTile(player, wallMapArray, 1, world, "every");

//If there's a collision, prevent the player from moving.
//Subtract its velocity from its position and then set its velocity to zero
if (!playerVsGround.hit) {
  player.cartX -= player.vx;
  player.cartY -= player.vy;
  player.vx = 0;
  player.vy = 0;
}
```

It's the same essential code we used to check for collisions in the maze game prototype from Chapter 3. Nothing new to learn!

Depth Layering

So far in these examples we've just been using flat diamond shaped sprites to build our isometric world. But in most games you'll want to use real, 3-dimensional-looking shapes for your sprites. Run the depthLayering.html file in this chapter's source files for a working example of just such an isometric world, shown in Figure 4-6.

Figure 4-6. *Build an isometric world using 3D sprites*

It's the same map, and uses the same keyboard control and collision as the previous examples. What's new is that the tiles are made from transparent cube images and are correctly depth sorted. Depth sorting means that the the sprites which appear closer to the viewer are displayed in-front of those that are further away.

Sorting a Sprite by Its z Property Value

There are two new things we need to add to our code to do proper isometric depth sorting. First, each of our sprites needs a new property called z, which determines its depth layer.

```
sprite.z = depthLayer;
```

Sprites on lower-level map layers should have a lower z value than those on higher-level map layers. You'll see in the code examples' heads how this value is found and assigned to sprites.

Next, you need to sort the sprites based on this new z value. Because most display systems draw sprites to the screen based on the order in which they appear in the display list, you can change their depth layer just by changing their order in the list. The display list is just an array of sprites, so that means all you need is a custom JavaScript array sort method to reorder the sprites in that array based on their z value.

Here's a custom sort function called byDepth that does just that. It works out each sprite's isometric depth by adding the sprite's Cartesian x and y position together, and multiplying it by its z value. It then shifts each pair of neighboring sprites in the array to a lower or higher index position based on its depth.

```
function byDepth(a, b) {

  //Calculate the depths of `a` and `b`
  //(add `1` to `a.z` and `b.x` to avoid multiplying by 0)
  a.depth = (a.cartX + a.cartY) * (a.z + 1);
  b.depth = (b.cartX + b.cartY) * (b.z + 1);

  //Move sprites with a lower depth to a higher position in the array
  if (a.depth < b.depth) {

    //Move the sprite down one position
    return -1;
  } else if (a.depth > b.depth) {

    //Move the sprite up one position
    return 1;
  } else {

    //Keep the sprite in the same position
    return 0;
  }
}
```

A return value of -1 means the sprite will be shifted down one place in the array, and a value of 1 means that it will be shifted up one place. A value of zero means the sprite will maintain its current position. To use the byDepth function, supply it as an argument to JavaScript's array sort method on any array that represents your sprite display list. Many scene graphs and game engines use an array called children that defines the display list, so you could sort the children array by depth like this:

```
world.children.sort(byDepth);
```

Now let's find out how to use this in practice.

Layering 3D Isometric Sprites

The depthLayering.js example file uses a tileset composed of three cube images, as shown in Figure 4-7.

Figure 4-7. *A tileset containing 3 isometric sprite images*

The green cube represents the maze walls, the red cube represents the player character, and the blue tile represents the floor. Each sprite is in its own map layer.

```
world.layers = [

  //The floor layer
  [
    1, 1, 1, 1, 1, 1, 1, 1,
    1, 1, 1, 1, 1, 1, 1, 1,
    1, 1, 1, 1, 1, 1, 1, 1,
    1, 1, 1, 1, 1, 1, 1, 1,
    1, 1, 1, 1, 1, 1, 1, 1,
    1, 1, 1, 1, 1, 1, 1, 1,
    1, 1, 1, 1, 1, 1, 1, 1,
    1, 1, 1, 1, 1, 1, 1, 1
  ],

  //The wall layer
  [
    2, 2, 2, 2, 2, 2, 2, 2,
    2, 0, 0, 0, 0, 0, 0, 2,
    2, 0, 2, 0, 0, 2, 0, 2,
    2, 0, 0, 0, 0, 2, 2, 2,
    2, 0, 0, 0, 0, 0, 0, 2,
    2, 2, 2, 0, 2, 0, 0, 2,
    2, 0, 0, 0, 0, 0, 0, 2,
    2, 2, 2, 2, 2, 2, 2, 2
  ],
```

```
//The player layer
[
  0, 0, 0, 0, 0, 0, 0, 0,
  0, 0, 0, 0, 0, 0, 0, 0,
  0, 0, 0, 0, 0, 0, 0, 0,
  0, 0, 0, 0, 0, 0, 0, 0,
  0, 0, 0, 0, 3, 0, 0, 0,
  0, 0, 0, 0, 0, 0, 0, 0,
  0, 0, 0, 0, 0, 0, 0, 0,
  0, 0, 0, 0, 0, 0, 0, 0
]
];
```

To help plot this map we need to initialize a new z value to help us track the depth of each layer. The z value is initialized to zero, and updated by one with each new layer. After each new sprite is created the z value is assigned to the sprite's own z property, so that we can properly depth sort it when the loop is finished.

```
//The `z` index
let z = 0;

//Build the game world by looping through each of the arrays
world.layers.forEach(layer => {

  //Loop through each array element
  layer.forEach((gid, index) => {

    //If the cell isn't empty (0) then create a sprite
    if (gid !== 0) {

      //Find the column and row that the sprite is on and also
      //its x and y pixel values
      let column, row, x, y;
      column = index % world.widthInTiles;
      row = Math.floor(index / world.widthInTiles);
      x = column * world.cartTilewidth;
      y = row * world.cartTileheight;

      //Next, create a different sprite based on what its
      //`gid` number is
      let sprite;
      switch (gid) {

        //The floor
        case 1:
          sprite = g.sprite(g.frame("images/isoTileset.png", 128, 0, 64, 64));
          break;

        //The walls
        case 2:
          sprite = g.sprite(g.frame("images/isoTileset.png", 0, 0, 64, 64));
          break;
```

```
    //The player
    case 3:
      sprite = g.sprite(g.frame("images/isoTileset.png", 64, 0, 64, 64));
      player = sprite;
      break;
  }

  //Add the isometric properties to the sprite
  addIsoProperties(sprite, x, y, world.cartTilewidth, world.cartTileheight);

  //Set the sprite's `x` and `y` pixel position based on its
  //isometric coordinates
  sprite.x = sprite.isoX;
  sprite.y = sprite.isoY;

  //Add the new `z` depth property to the sprite
  sprite.z = z;

  //Add the sprite to the `world` container
  world.addChild(sprite);
  }
});

//Add `1` to `z` for each new layer
z += 1;
});

//Move the player into the environment's depth layer
player.z = 1;

//Sort the world by depth
world.children.sort(byDepth);
```

The last two lines in the code above are important. After the loop runs, the floor sprites will have a z value of 0, the walls will have a z value of 1, and the player character (the red cube) will have a z value of 2. However, we want the player character to be at the same depth level as the walls, so we need to manually set the player's z property to 1. If we'd left it at the original value of 2, the player would appear to float on a layer above the walls. The last thing the code does is depth sort the world object's children array so that the player sprite is organized into the correct layer.

Updating Depths

Whenever any of the sprites change their positions, they need to be depth sorted again. In this example's game loop the player sprite is being moved around using the keyboard. Each time it moves, all the sprites in the world object's children array need to be re-sorted.

```
if (player.vx !== 0 || player.vy !== 0) {
  world.children.sort(byDepth);
}
```

Sorting an array is a computationally expensive thing to do, so you only want to do it when you absolutely have to. That's why the code above only does it when the player sprite's velocity has changed.

Making Isometric Maps with Tiled Editor

If you're making a big, complex isometric map, it's far easier to use a tool like Tiled Editor to do it than to program your map layer arrays by hand. Tiled Editor has built-in support for isometric maps, and we can use its output to easily generate any kind of isometric world. We just need to configure Tiled Editor in the right way and make some small changes to our makeTiledWorld function from Chapter 2.

Run the cubes.html, shown in Figure 4-8, for an example of a game prototype designed with the help of Tiled Editor. It runs very much like our previous example, including keyboard movement, collision, and depth layering.

index: 21

Figure 4-8. *An isometric game prototype built using Tiled Editor*

Let's find out how you can used Tiled Editor to build something like this yourself.

Configuring and Building the Map

Before you start creating your Tiled Editor map, prepare a sprite sheet with the isometric tiles that you want to use. And, very importantly, note down the isometric dimensions of sprites. Here are the pixel dimensions you need to know:

- tilewidth: The width of the sprite, from its left to right edge.

- tileheight: The height of the tile's *base area*. This is just the height of the squashed diamond shape that defines the base on which the isometric sprite is standing. Usually it's half the tilewidth value.

Figure 4-9 illustrates how to find these values.

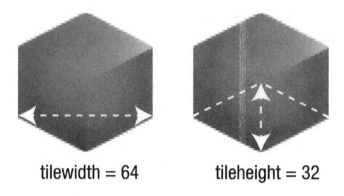

tilewidth = 64   tileheight = 32

Figure 4-9. *The tilewidth and tileheight property values*

These properties are the property names that are used by Tiled Editor, and you'll be able to access them in the JSON data file that Tiled Editor generates.

■ **Note**   The property names `tilewidth` and `tileheight` are what Tiled Editor uses and generates for the JSON file. So, for consistency I've maintained the same names and capitalization.

You can now use the values to create a new isometric map in Tiled Editor. Open Tiled Editor and select File ➤ New from the main menu. In the New Map dialogue box, select `isometric` as the Orientation, and use the `tilewidth` and `tileheight` values I described above for the `Width` and `Height`. Figure 4-10 shows an example.

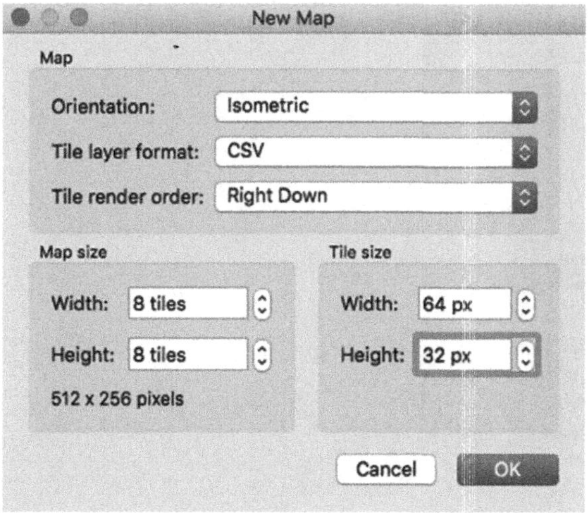

Figure 4-10. *Create a new isometric map in Tiled Editor*

But we're not done yet! There are three more values we need to figure out:

- `tileDepth`: The total height of the isometric sprite, in pixels. Figure 4-11 illustrates this value.

tileDepth = 64

Figure 4-11. *The tileDepth property describes the total height of the isometric sprite*

- `cartWidth`: The Cartesian width of each tile grid cell, in pixels.
- `cartHeight`: The Cartesian height of each tile grid cell, in pixels.

You need to add these values as custom properties in Tiled Editor's Map Properties panel. Figure 4-12 shows what this should look like.

Property	Value
Height	8
Tile Width	64
Tile Height	32
Tile Side Length (Hex)	0
Stagger Axis	Y
Stagger Index	Odd
Tile Layer Format	CSV
Tile Render Order	Right Down
▶ Background Color	■ [128, 128, 128] (255)
▼ Custom Properties	
cartTileheight	32
cartTilewidth	32
tileDepth	64

Figure 4-12. *Add custom map properties*

When Tiled Editor generates the JSON map data, you'll be able to access these values in the properties field.

```
"properties":
    {
      "cartTileheight":"32",
      "cartTilewidth":"32",
      "tileDepth":"64"
    },
```

You'll see in the code examples ahead how we'll need to uses these values to accurately plot the isometric map.

Now that you've got the Map Properties all set up, use your isometric tileset to build your world, just like you did in Chapter 2. Figure 4-13 shows an example of what your Tiled Editor workspace might look like.

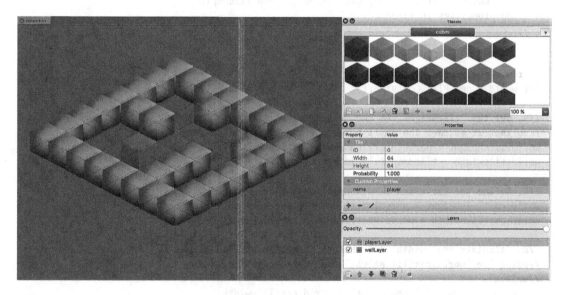

Figure 4-13. *Designing an isometric map in Tiled Editor*

You can see in Figure 4-13 that I've given the red cube a custom name property with the value "player," I've also built the map using two layers: the playerLayer just contains the red cube, and the wallLayer contains all the maze walls.

When you're finished designing your map, export it as a JSON file, and you're now ready to use it to start coding a game.

The makeIsoTiledWorld Function

The next step is to modify our makeTiledWorld function from Chapter 2 so that it works with with isometric maps. Here's the new makeIsoTiledWorld that does this. It follows the same format as the original, but applies everything we've learned about isometric maps in this chapter. I've added comments to the code, listed from A to I, that highlight the new modifications.

```
function makeIsoTiledWorld(jsonTiledMap, tileset) {

  //Create a group called `world` to contain all the layers, sprites
  //and objects from the `tiledMap`. The `world` object is going to be
  //returned to the main game program
  let tiledMap = PIXI.loader.resources[jsonTiledMap].data;

  //A. You need to add three custom properties to your Tiled Editor
  //map: `cartTilewidth`,`cartTileheight` and `tileDepth`.
  //Check to make sure that these custom properties exist
  if (!tiledMap.properties.cartTilewidth
  && !tiledMap.properties.cartTileheight
  && !tiledMao.properties.tileDepth) {
    throw new Error(
      "Set custom cartTilewidth, cartTileheight and tileDepth
      map properties in Tiled Editor"
    );
  }

  //Create the `world` container
  let world = new PIXI.Container();

  //B. Set the `tileHeight` to the `tiledMap`'s `tileDepth` property
  //so that it matches the pixel height of the sprite tile image
  world.tileheight = parseInt(tiledMap.properties.tileDepth);
  world.tilewidth = tiledMap.tilewidth;

  //C. Define the Cartesian dimesions of each tile
  world.cartTileheight = parseInt(tiledMap.properties.cartTileheight);
  world.cartTilewidth = parseInt(tiledMap.properties.cartTilewidth);

  //D. Calculate the `width` and `height` of the world, in pixels
  //using the `world.cartTileHeight` and `world.cartTilewidth`
  //values
  world.worldWidth = tiledMap.width * world.cartTilewidth;
  world.worldHeight = tiledMap.height * world.cartTileheight;

  //Get a reference to the world's height and width in
  //tiles, in case you need to know this later (you will!)
  world.widthInTiles = tiledMap.width;
  world.heightInTiles = tiledMap.height;

  //Create an `objects` array to store references to any
  //named objects in the map. Named objects all have
  //a `name` property that was assigned in Tiled Editor
  world.objects = [];

  //The optional spacing (padding) around each tile
  //This is to account for spacing around tiles
```

```
//that's commonly used with texture atlas tilesets. Set the
//`spacing` property when you create a new map in Tiled Editor
let spacing = tiledMap.tilesets[0].spacing;

//Figure out how many columns there are on the tileset.
//This is the width of the image, divided by the width
//of each tile, plus any optional spacing thats around each tile
let numberOfTilesetColumns =
  Math.floor(
    tiledMap.tilesets[0].imagewidth / (tiledMap.tilewidth + spacing)
  );

//E. A `z` property to help track which depth level the sprites are on
let z = 0;

//Loop through all the map layers
tiledMap.layers.forEach(tiledLayer => {

  //Make a group for this layer and copy
  //all of the layer properties onto it
  let layerGroup = new PIXI.Container();

  Object.keys(tiledLayer).forEach(key => {

    //Add all the layer's properties to the group, except the
    //width and height (because the group will work those our for
    //itself based on its content)
    if (key !== "width" && key !== "height") {
      layerGroup[key] = tiledLayer[key];
    }
  });

  //Translate `opacity` to `alpha`
  layerGroup.alpha = tiledLayer.opacity;

  //Add the group to the `world`
  world.addChild(layerGroup);

  //Push the group into the world's `objects` array
  //So you can access it later
  world.objects.push(layerGroup);

  //Is this current layer a `tilelayer`?
  if (tiledLayer.type === "tilelayer") {

    //Loop through the `data` array of this layer
    tiledLayer.data.forEach((gid, index) => {
      let tileSprite, texture, mapX, mapY, tilesetX, tilesetY,
        mapColumn, mapRow, tilesetColumn, tilesetRow;
```

```
//If the grid id number (`gid`) isn't zero, create a sprite
if (gid !== 0) {

  //Figure out the map column and row number that we're on, and then
  //calculate the grid cell's x and y pixel position
  mapColumn = index % world.widthInTiles;
  mapRow = Math.floor(index / world.widthInTiles);

  //F. Use the Cartesian values to find the
  //`mapX` and `mapY` values
  mapX = mapColumn * world.cartTilewidth;
  mapY = mapRow * world.cartTileheight;

  //Figure out the column and row number that the tileset
  //image is on, and then use those values to calculate
  //the x and y pixel position of the image on the tileset
  tilesetColumn = ((gid - 1) % numberOfTilesetColumns);
  tilesetRow = Math.floor((gid - 1) / numberOfTilesetColumns);
  tilesetX = tilesetColumn * world.tilewidth;
  tilesetY = tilesetRow * world.tileheight;

  //Compensate for any optional spacing (padding) around the tiles if
  //there is any. This bit of code accumlates the spacing offsets from the
  //left side of the tileset and adds them to the current tile's position
  if (spacing > 0) {
    tilesetX
      += spacing + (spacing * ((gid - 1) % numberOfTilesetColumns));
    tilesetY
      += spacing + (spacing * Math.floor((gid - 1) / numberOfTilesetColumns));
  }

  //Use the above values to create the sprite's image from
  //the tileset image
  texture = g.frame(
    tileset, tilesetX, tilesetY,
    world.tilewidth, world.tileheight
  );

  //I've dedcided that any tiles that have a `name` property are important
  //and should be accessible in the `world.objects` array

  let tileproperties = tiledMap.tilesets[0].tileproperties,
    key = String(gid - 1);

  //If the JSON `tileproperties` object has a sub-object that
  //matches the current tile, and that sub-object has a `name` property,
  //then create a sprite and assign the tile properties onto
  //the sprite
  if (tileproperties[key] && tileproperties[key].name) {

    //Make a sprite
    tileSprite = new PIXI.Sprite(texture);
```

```
        //Copy all of the tile's properties onto the sprite
        //(This includes the `name` property)
        Object.keys(tileproperties[key]).forEach(property => {

          tileSprite[property] = tileproperties[key][property];
        });

        //Push the sprite into the world's `objects` array
        //so that you can access it by `name` later
        world.objects.push(tileSprite);
      }

      //If the tile doesn't have a `name` property, just use it to
      //create an ordinary sprite (it will only need one texture)
      else {
        tileSprite = new PIXI.Sprite(texture);
      }

      //G. Add isometric properties to the sprite
      addIsoProperties(
        tileSprite, mapX, mapY,
        world.cartTilewidth, world.cartTileheight
      );

      //H. Use the isometric position to add the sprite to the world
      tileSprite.x = tileSprite.isoX;
      tileSprite.y = tileSprite.isoY;
      tileSprite.z = z;

      //Make a record of the sprite's index number in the array
      //(We'll use this for collision detection later)
      tileSprite.index = index;

      //Make a record of the sprite's `gid` on the tileset.
      //This will also be useful for collision detection later
      tileSprite.gid = gid;

      //Add the sprite to the current layer group
      layerGroup.addChild(tileSprite);
    }
  });
}

//Is this layer an `objectgroup`?
if (tiledLayer.type === "objectgroup") {
  tiledLayer.objects.forEach(object => {

    //We're just going to capture the object's properties
    //so that we can decide what to do with it later.
    //Get a reference to the layer group the object is in
    object.group = layerGroup;
```

```
    //Push the object into the world's `objects` array
    world.objects.push(object);
  });
}


//I. Add 1 to the z index (the first layer will have a z index of `1`)
  z += 1;
});


//Search functions

world.getObject = (objectName) => {
  let searchForObject = () => {
    let foundObject;
    world.objects.some(object => {
      if (object.name && object.name === objectName) {
        foundObject = object;
        return true;
      }
    });
    if (foundObject) {
      return foundObject;
    } else {
      throw new Error("There is no object with the property name: " + objectName);
    }
  };


  //Return the search function
  return searchForObject();
};

  world.getObjects = (objectNames) => {
    let foundObjects = [];
    world.objects.forEach(object => {
      if (object.name && objectNames.indexOf(object.name) !== -1) {
        foundObjects.push(object);
      }
    });
    if (foundObjects.length > 0) {
      return foundObjects;
    } else {
      throw new Error("I could not find those objects");
    }
    return foundObjects;
  };

  //That's it, we're done!
  //Finally, return the `world` object back to the game program
  return world;
}
```

With this new `makeIsoTiledWorld` function we've got a way to plot the the map we we created in Tiled Editor and access all the sprites it contains. Let's find out exactly how to do that next.

Building the Game World

Using the `makeIsoTiledWorld` function works just like our original `makeTiledWorld` function, so there's really nothing new to learn. The only thing you need to keep in mind is that if you change the position or z property of any sprite, you need to re-sort the sprites using our custom `byDepth` function. In this case, all our sprites are in the `children` array of each map layer container, so you need to depth sort them like this:

```
mapLayer.children.sort(byDepth);
```

Apart from this, there's nothing new to learn. Here's the complete application code for the cubes.js file, which was illustrated in Figure 4-8. It loads up the isometric map that was created in Tiled Editor, adds keyboard interactivity, collision and accurate depth sorting. You've see all this code before in other contexts, and the comments explain the details.

```
//The files we want to load
let thingsToLoad = [
  "images/cubes.png",
  "images/cubes.json"
];

//Create a new Hexi instance, and start it
let g = hexi(512, 512, setup, thingsToLoad);

//Scale the canvas to the maximum browser dimensions
g.scaleToWindow();

//Declare variables used in more than one function
let world, leftArrow, upArrow,
  rightArrow, downArrow, message, wallLayer,
  player, wallMapArray;

//Start Hexi
g.start();

function setup() {

  //Make the world from the Tiled JSON data
  world = makeIsoTiledWorld(
    "images/cubes.json",
    "images/cubes.png"
  );

  //Add the world to the `stage`
  g.stage.addChild(world);

  //Position the world inside the canvas
  let canvasOffset = (g.canvas.width / 2) - world.tilewidth / 2;
  world.x += canvasOffset;
  world.y = 0;
```

```
//Get the objects we need from the world
player = world.getObject("player");
wallLayer = world.getObject("wallLayer");

//Add the player to the wall layer and set it at
//the same depth level as the walls
wallLayer.addChild(player);
player.z = 0;
wallLayer.children.sort(byDepth);

//Initialize the player's velocity to zero
player.vx = 0;
player.vy = 0;

//Make a text object
message = g.text("", "16px Futura", "black");
message.setPosition(5, 0);

//Create the keyboard objects
leftArrow = g.keyboard(37);
upArrow = g.keyboard(38);
rightArrow = g.keyboard(39);
downArrow = g.keyboard(40);

//Assign the key `press` actions
player.direction = "none";
leftArrow.press = () => player.direction = "left";
upArrow.press = () => player.direction = "up";
rightArrow.press = () => player.direction = "right";
downArrow.press = () => player.direction = "down";
leftArrow.release = () => player.direction = "none";
upArrow.release = () => player.direction = "none";
rightArrow.release = () => player.direction = "none";
downArrow.release = () => player.direction = "none";

//Set the game state to `play`
  g.state = play;
}

function play() {

  //Change the player character's velocity if it's centered over a grid cell
  if (Math.floor(player.cartX) % world.cartTilewidth === 0
  && Math.floor(player.cartY) % world.cartTileheight === 0) {
    switch (player.direction) {
      case "up":
        player.vy = -2;
        player.vx = 0;
        break;
```

```
      case "down":
        player.vy = 2;
        player.vx = 0;
        break;
      case "left":
        player.vx = -2;
        player.vy = 0;
        break;
      case "right":
        player.vx = 2;
        player.vy = 0;
        break;
      case "none":
        player.vx = 0;
        player.vy = 0;
        break;
    }
}

//Update the player's Cartesian position, based on its velocity
player.cartY += player.vy;
player.cartX += player.vx;

//Wall collision
//Get a reference to the wall map array
wallMapArray = wallLayer.data;

//Use `hitTestIsoTile` to check for a collision
let playerVsGround = hitTestIsoTile(player, wallMapArray, 0, world, "every");

//If there's a collision, prevent the player from moving.
//Subtract its velocity from its position and then set its velocity to zero
if (!playerVsGround.hit) {
  player.cartX -= player.vx;
  player.cartY -= player.vy;
  player.vx = 0;
  player.vy = 0;
}

//Add world boundaries
let top = 0,
  bottom = (world.heightInTiles * world.cartTileheight),
  left = 0,
  right = (world.widthInTiles * world.cartTilewidth);

//Prevent the player from crossing any of the world boundaries
//Top
if (player.cartY < 0) {
  player.cartY = top;
}
```

```
//Bottom
if (player.cartY + player.cartHeight > bottom) {
  player.cartY = bottom - player.cartHeight;
}
```

```
//Left
if (player.cartX < left) {
  player.cartX = left;
}
```

```
//Right
if (player.cartX + player.cartWidth > right) {
  player.cartX = right - player.cartWidth;
}
```

```
//Position the sprite's screen `x` and `y` position
//using its isometric coordinates
player.x = player.isoX;
player.y = player.isoY;
```

```
//Get the player's index position in the map array
player.index = g.getIndex(
  player.cartX, player.cartY,
  world.cartTilewidth, world.cartTileheight, world.widthInTiles
);
```

```
//Depth sort the sprites if the player is moving
if (player.vx !== 0 || player.vy !== 0) {
  wallLayer.children.sort(byDepth);
}
```

```
//Display the player's x, y and index values
  message.content = `index: ${player.index}`;
}
```

Summary

Whether your game is displayed using Cartesian or isometric projection, the underlying logic behind working with tile-based games is the same. As you've seen in this chapter, if you know how to plot maps, add keyboard interactivity, and do collision detection using Cartesian coordinates, you can apply that same logic to isometric maps, with the addition of two simple little conversion formulas. You've also learned how to apply these formulas to pointer position coordinates so that you can accurately select isometric sprites on the screen. And, you've learned how to create and plot isometric maps using Tiled Editor, and accurately depth sort those sprites using z values so that they display in their correct depth layers. These are all the basic skills you need to start making a wide variety of isometric games, from strategy games to dungeon crawlers.

Now that you know how to make all sorts of interactive tile-based game environments, how can you create game characters that are able to intelligently navigate through those environments? That's what the next chapter is all about: pathfinding.

CHAPTER 5

■ ■ ■

Pathfinding Basics

You now know how to make a tile-based game world, and you also know how to make a player character that can navigate through that world. But how do you create sprites that can wander around and explore the world on their own? Take a moment to play the example prototype called tileBasedLineOfSight.html that you'll find in this chapter's source files (shown in Figure 5-1). The maze is populated by three monsters who wander around randomly until they spot the alien character – then they chase him relentlessly.

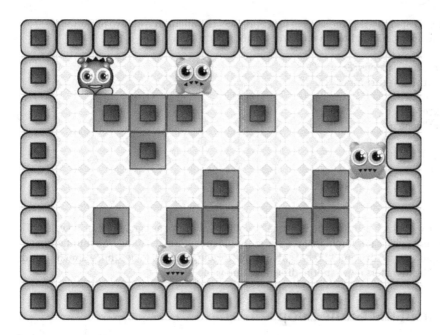

Figure 5-1. *The monsters navigate the game world autonomously and chase the player character*

The monsters seem to have a kind of intelligence, and behave much as you would expect living creatures to behave. But, of course, it's just an effective illusion, thanks to a collection of game programming techniques broadly known as **pathfinding**: how to make sprites that can autonomously interpret and navigate a game world. In this chapter you're going to learn all the basics of pathfinding, including:

- How to analyze and interpret the environment that a sprite is in.

- Random movement through a maze.

- Finding the closest direction to a target.

- Line of sight: How to know if a sprite can see another sprite.

Pathfinding is actually a rudimentary form of Artificial Intelligence (AI), and you'll be able to apply these techniques, not just to a wide range of different games, but any programming problem where you need to interpret the meaning of some data based on its context in a larger set of data. And, it's pretty easy to do! So let's start with some pathfinding fundamentals, and go from there.

Random Movement Through a Maze

The best place to start with pathfinding is to first create sprites that move around a maze at random. Run the randomMovement.html file and you'll find a simpler version of the same maze game shown in Figure 5-1. Instead of actively searching for the alien character, the monsters change their direction randomly whenever they're at an intersection. Let's go on a tour of how this code works, and we'll learn all the pathfinding basics as we go.

Direction and Speed

When monster sprites are created in the game's setup function, they're initialized with two important properties: direction and speed, highlighted in the sprite creation code below:

```
monsters = mapMonsters.map(mapMonster => {
  let monster = g.sprite(monsterFrames);
  monster.x = mapMonster.x;
  monster.y = mapMonster.y;
  monster.direction = "none";
  monster.speed = 4;
  monsterLayer.addChild(monster);
  mapMonster.visible = false;
  return monster;
});
```

The direction is a string, which is initialized to "none" – you'll see how we assign it new string values ahead. speed is the number of pixels per frame that the sprite should move, and it should be a number that divides evenly into the map's tilewidth and tileheight size. We're going to need to use those direction and speed values to help give the monsters new random directions and velocities.

Moving the Sprite in the Game Loop

The code that actually chooses the monsters' new direction and makes them move runs inside the game loop. The code that does this needs to do four important things:

1. Find out if the monster is centered directly over a map tile cell.

2. If it is, choose a new random direction.

3. Use the monster's new random direction and speed to find its velocity.

4. Use the new velocity to move the monster.

Here's the code from the game loop that does all this.

```
monsters.forEach(monster => {

  //1. Is the monster directly centered over a map tile cell?
  if (isCenteredOverCell(monster)) {

    //2. Yes, it is, so find out which are valid directions to move.
    //`validDirections` returns an array which can include any
    //of these string values: "up", "right", "down"or "left" or
    monster.validDirections = validDirections(
      monster, wallMapArray, 0, world
    );

    //3. Can the monster change its direction?
    if (canChangeDirection(monster.validDirections)) {

      //4. If it can, randomly select a new direction from the monsters valid directions
      monster.direction = randomDirection(monster, monster.validDirections);
    }

    //5. Use the monster's direction and speed to find its new velocity
    let velocity = directionToVelocity(monster.direction, monster.speed);
    monster.vx = velocity.vx;
    monster.vy = velocity.vy;
  }

  //6. Move the monster
  monster.x += monster.vx;
  monster.y += monster.vy;
});
```

This is very high-level code. You can see that all the important functionality is hidden away in five important functions: isCenteredOverCell, validDirections, canChangeDirection, randomDirection, and directionToVelocity. We're going to look at each of these functions, in turn, to find out exactly how they work.

Is the Sprite Centered Over a Tile Cell?

As you learned in Chapter 3, your sprites will move with more accuracy and precision in a tile-based world if they only change direction when they're exactly centered over a cell. So the first thing the code does if figure this out by using a helper function called isCenteredOverCell. Supply it with a sprite, and isCenteredOverCell will return true if the sprite is centered, and false if it isn't.

```
function isCenteredOverCell(sprite) {
  return Math.floor(sprite.x) % world.tilewidth === 0
  && Math.floor(sprite.y) % world.tileheight === 0
}
```

This is a funky bit of boiler plate code that shows how unexpectedly useful the modulus operator (%) can sometimes be. (As a reminder, the modulus operator tells you what the remainder is of a division operation.) The code above finds out if the x and y top-left corner position of the sprite, divided by the width and height of the tile, has a remainder of zero. If it does, then you know the sprite is at an x/y location that divides absolutely evenly into the dimensions of the tile. And, that can only mean one thing: that the sprite is *exactly* aligned over the cell. It's a clever trick – thank you, modulus operator!

If the sprite is centered, the next step is to find out which are the possible valid directions that the sprite can choose.

Finding the Valid Directions

The validDirections function analyzes the map environment that the sprite is currently in, and returns an array of strings with all possible valid directions that the sprite can move in.

```
monster.validDirections = validDirections(
  monster,        //The sprite
  wallMapArray,   //The tile map array
  0,              //The gid value that represents an empty tile
  world           //The world object. It needs these properties:
                  //`tilewidth`, `tileheight` and `widthInTiles`
);
```

The array that validDirections returns can include any of these five string values: "up", "down", "left", "right", or "none." How it figures this out is quite interesting, so let's first take a look at the entire validDirections function, and then I'll walk you through how it works, step by step.

```
function validDirections(sprite, mapArray, validGid, world) {

  //Get the sprite's current map index position number
  let index = g.getIndex(
    sprite.x,
    sprite.y,
    world.tilewidth,
    world.tileheight,
    world.widthInTiles
  );

  //An array containing the index numbers of tile cells
  //above, below and to the left and right of the sprite
  let surroundingCrossCells = (index, widthInTiles) => {
    return [
      index - widthInTiles,    //Cell above
      index - 1,               //Cell to the left
      index + 1,               //Cell to the right
      index + widthInTiles,    //Cell below
    ];
  };

  //Get the index position numbers of the 4 cells to the top, right, left
  //and bottom of the sprite
  let surroundingIndexNumbers = surroundingCrossCells(index, world.widthInTiles);
```

```
//Find all the tile gid numbers that match the surrounding index numbers
let surroundingTileGids = surroundingIndexNumbers.map(index => {
  return mapArray[index];
});

//`directionList` is an array of 4 string values that can be either
//"up", "left", "right", "down" or "none", depending on
//whether there is a cell with a valid gid that matches that direction
let directionList = surroundingTileGids.map((gid, i) => {

  //The possible directions
  let possibleDirections = ["up", "left", "right", "down"];

  //If the direction is valid, choose the matching string
  //identifier for that direction. Otherwise, return "none"
  if (gid === validGid) {
    return possibleDirections[i];
  } else {
    return "none";
  }
});

//We don't need "none" in the list of directions, so
//let's filter it out (it's just a placeholder)
let filteredDirectionList = directionList.filter(direction => direction != "none");

//Return the filtered list of valid directions
return filteredDirectionList;
}
```

Now let's find out how this actually works!

The Tiles Surrounding the Sprite

The first thing the validDirections function does is to figure out which map tiles are surrounding the sprite. A function called surroundingCrossCells uses the sprite's index number in the map array to figure this out. It returns an array of four map index numbers that represent the cells above, to the left, to the right, and below the sprite.

```
let surroundingCrossCells = (index, widthInTiles) => {
  return [
    index - widthInTiles,    //Cell above
    index - 1,               //Cell to the left
    index + 1,               //Cell to the right
    index + widthInTiles,    //Cell below
  ];
};

let surroundingIndexNumbers =
  surroundingCrossCells(index, world.widthInTiles);
```

Figure 5-2 illustrates where these cells are in relation to the sprite, and their matching map array index numbers. In this example there are 11 cells in each row of this maze and the monster sprite's position index number is 38. The map array index numbers surrounding the sprite, starting at the top and going clockwise, are 27, 39, 49, and 37.

Figure 5-2. *Find the cells surrounding the sprite*

We now have an array called surroundingIndexNumbers that tells us the index numbers of the cells around the sprite. But that's not enough information; we also need to know what gid values of those cells are, so that we know what kind of tiles they contain. Remember, we want to allow the sprite to move to empty tiles, but prevent it from moving to wall tiles. So the next step is then to use those index numbers to find out exactly which tile sprites are at those locations. Let's map the surroundingIndexNumbers to a new array that tells us the actual gid numbers of those cells. Here's how:

```
let surroundingTileGids = surroundingIndexNumbers.map(index => {
  return mapArray[index];
});
```

For example, the index numbers from Figure 5-2, 27, 39, 49, and 35 would now map to a new array containing the following gid values: 0, 0, 2, and 0. The number 0 represents an empty cell, and the number 2 represents a wall. Figure 5-3 illustrates this.

Figure 5-3. *Find out what kinds of tiles are in the surrounding cells by getting their gid numbers*

The Valid Directions

The next step is to give direction names, as strings, to each of the four possible directions that the sprite can move to. The direction names can be any of the following: "up." "left," "right," "down," or "none." The following bit of code maps our surroundingTileGids array to a new array called directionList, which contains these direction strings.

```
let directionList = surroundingTileGids.map((gid, i) => {

  //The possible directions
  let possibleDirections = ["up", "left", "right", "down"];

  //If the direction is valid, choose the matching string
  //identifier for that direction. Otherwise, return "none"
  if (gid === validGid) {
    return possibleDirections[i];
  } else {
    return "none";
  }
});
```

Any gid that isn't valid is given the direction name "none." Figure 5-4 illustrates the resulting array produced by the directionList function.

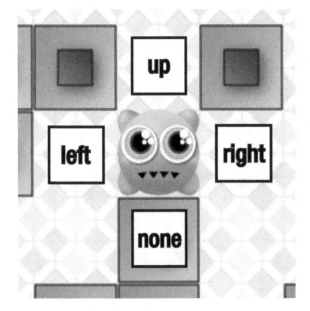

Figure 5-4. *Find the direction names*

We don't actually need the "none" value, so let's filter it out (it's just acting as a placeholder):

```
let filteredDirectionList = directionList.filter(direction => {
  return direction != "none"
});
```

filteredDirectionList is now our final array, which contains all the valid directions in which the sprite can move:

```
["up", "left", "right"]
```

(Or, if the sprite is completely trapped on all sides, this array will be empty – but we'll get to that!)

This array is returned by the validDirections function, which completes the first major step in the pathfinding process.

Can the Monster Change Direction?

There are actually only certain places on the map where the monsters should change their directions.

- When they're in a passage intersection.

- If they're in a cul-de-sac (a dead end).

- Or if they're trapped by walls on all four sides (in which case they should stop moving completely).

The X's in Figure 5-5 mark where these three map conditions are in the maze we're using.

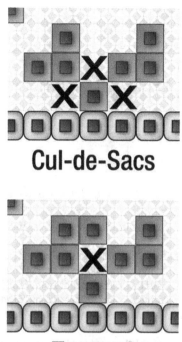

Cul-de-Sacs

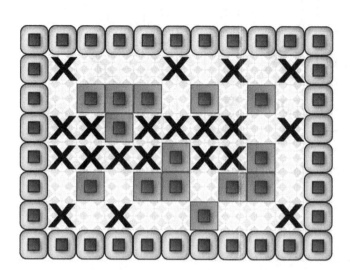

Passage intersections

Trapped

Figure 5-5. *Find the direction names*

If the monsters are not at a map location that matches one of these conditions, they'll just continue on in their current directions.

It's easy to figure these out what the monster's current map location type is. If the there are no elements in the validDirections array, then you know that the sprite is trapped.

```
let trapped = validDirections.length === 0;
```

You know that a sprite is in a cul-de-sac if there's just one element in the validDirections array.

```
let inCulDeSac = validDirections.length === 1;
```

Those were easy, but now how do we know if a sprite is at a passage intersection? First, ask yourself, "What is a passage intersection?" Take a close look at Figure 5-5, and ask yourself what values might be in the validDirections array if a sprite were at any of the map positions marked with an X. Any ideas? Yes, that's right! A passage intersection will always contain the values "left" or "right" *and* "up" or "down." Figure 5-6 illustrates this.

Figure 5-6. *Passage intersections always contain a left/right value and an up/down vlaue*

Here's how you can express this in code:

```
let up = validDirections.find(x => x === "up"),
    down = validDirections.find(x => x === "down"),
    left = validDirections.find(x => x === "left"),
    right = validDirections.find(x => x === "right"),
    atIntersection = (up || down) && (left || right);
```

If atIntersection is true, you know that the sprite is at one of the passage intersections marked by an X. Easy!

We now know how to tell if a sprite is trapped, in a cul-de-sac, or at a passage intersection. So let's wrap all this code into a bigger function called canChangeDirection. It will return return true if any of these conditions are true, or false if they aren't.

```
function canChangeDirection(validDirections = []) {

  //Is the sprite in a dead-end (cul de sac.) This will be true if there's only
  //one element in the `validDirections` array
  let inCulDeSac = validDirections.length === 1;

  //Is the sprite trapped? This will be true if there are no elements in
  //the `validDirections` array
  let trapped = validDirections.length === 0;

  //Is the sprite in a passage? This will be `true` if the the sprite
  //is at a location that contain the values
  //"left" or "right" and "up" or "down"
  let up = validDirections.find(x => x === "up"),
      down = validDirections.find(x => x === "down"),
      left = validDirections.find(x => x === "left"),
      right = validDirections.find(x => x === "right"),
      atIntersection = (up || down) && (left || right);

  //Return `true` if the sprite can change direction or `false` if it can't
  return trapped || atIntersection || inCulDeSac;
}
```

Now that we have a way to tell if a sprite is at a map location where it can change direction, let's find out how to give it a new random direction.

Choosing a Random Direction

Now that we know what the sprite's valid directions are, all we have to do is pick one at random. The randomDirection function randomly returns a single string from the validDirections array: "up," "left," "right," or "down." If there are no valid directions it means the sprite is trapped on all sides, and the function returns the string "trapped." Here's the randomDirection array that does this:

```
function randomDirection(sprite, validDirections = []) {

  //The `randomInt` helper function returns a random integer between a minimum
  //and maximum value
  let randomInt = (min, max) => {
    return Math.floor(Math.random() * (max - min + 1)) + min;
  };

  //Is the sprite trapped?
  let trapped = validDirections.length === 0;

  //If the sprite isn't trapped, randomly choose one of the valid
  //directions. Otherwise, return the string "trapped"
  if (!trapped) {
    return validDirections[randomInt(0, validDirections.length - 1)];
  } else {
    return "trapped"
  }
}
```

Converting the Direction String to a Velocity Number

We now know which direction the sprite should move in. But, for that information to be useful to move a sprite, we need to convert the direction string into a number that represents the sprite's velocity. A function called directionToVelocity does that job: it returns an object with vx and vy properties that correspond to the direction the sprite should move.

```
function directionToVelocity(direction = "", speed = 0) {
  switch (direction) {
    case "up":
      return {
        vy: -speed,
        vx: 0
      }
      break;
    case "down":
      return {
        vy: speed,
        vx: 0
      };
      break;
```

111

```
      case "left":
        return {
          vx: -speed,
          vy: 0
        };
        break;
      case "right":
        return {
          vx: speed,
          vy: 0
        };
        break;
      default:
        return {
          vx: 0,
          vy: 0
        };
    }
};
```

If the monster's direction is "trapped," the default case will be triggered and vx and vy values, which represent the monster's speed, will be zero.

To make the sprite move, update the sprite's velocity with these values:

```
let velocity = directionToVelocity(monster.direction, monster.speed);
monster.vx = velocity.vx;
monster.vy = velocity.vy;
```

And then apply them to the sprite's current position:

```
monster.x += monster.vx;
monster.y += monster.vy;
```

And that's how to make a monster randomly move around a maze!

Hunting the Alien

Randomly moving monsters are a good start, but for a more challenging game you'll want your monsters to actively seek out and hunt the player character. Run the closestDirection.html file in this chapter's source files for an interactive example of just such a system, illustrated in Figure 5-7.

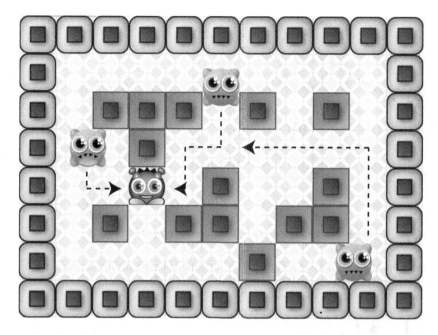

Figure 5-7. *The monsters always choose the closest direction to the player character*

No matter where they are in the maze, the monsters will always choose to move in a direction that takes them closer to the player character.

Calculating the Vector

To make this work, you need to know which of the monsters' four possible directions are closest to the alien. The first step is to draw a *vector* between the center points of a monster and the alien. A vector is just an invisible mathematical line that, among its many uses, can be used to figure out the distance and angle between two sprites. A vector is represented by two values, vx and vy, and you can calculate a vector between two sprites like this:

```
let vx = spriteTwo.centerX - spriteOne.centerX,
    vy = spriteTwo.centerY - spriteOne.centerY;
```

vx tells us the distance between the objects on the X axis. vy tells us the distance between the objects on the Y axis. The vx and vy variables together describe a vector between the objects.

The vector is just a mathematical representation of a line – you don't actually see it displayed on the screen. But, if you could see it, it might look something like the black diagonal line that runs between the centers of the two sprites in Figure 5-8.

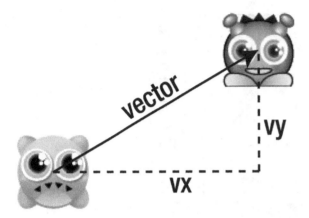

Figure 5-8. *A vector can help you figure out the distance and angle between two sprites*

To make the monster hunt the alien, we have to move it in the horizontal or vertical direction with the *greatest amount of distance* between it and the alien. Why is that? Take a look at Figure 5-9.

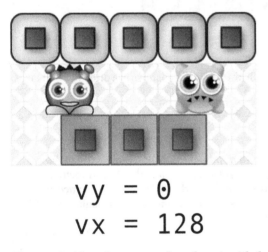

$$vy = 0$$
$$vx = 128$$

Figure 5-9. *Move the monster along the axis with the greatest distance between the sprites*

It's obvious that the monster should choose the left direction along the X axis if it wants to get closer to the player. However, the X axis is also the one with the greatest distance between the objects. Unintuitive, but true!

Now that we know this, we can use a simple if/else statement to tell us which direction is the closest direction to the target: "up," "down," "left," or "right." Here's a function called `closest` that wraps this all up and returns the correct value for us:

```
let closest = () => {

  //Plot a vector between spriteTwo and spriteOne
  let vx = spriteTwo.centerX - spriteOne.centerX,
      vy = spriteTwo.centerY - spriteOne.centerY;
```

```
//If the distance is greater on the X axis...
if (Math.abs(vx) >= Math.abs(vy)) {

  //Try left and right
  if (vx <= 0) {
    return "left";
  } else {
    return "right";
  }
}

//If the distance is greater on the Y axis...
else {

  //Try up and down
  if (vy <= 0) {
    return "up"
  } else {
    return "down"
  }
}
};
```

Now let's find out how to integrate this with our existing code.

Finding the Closest Direction

Open the closesestDirection.js file in the chapter's source files and you'll find this bit of code in the play function (the game loop) that's responsible for moving the monsters and choosing their new directions. It's identical to the code we used at the beginning of the chapter, except for step number 4.

```
monsters.forEach(monster => {

  //1. Is the monster directly centered over a map tile cell?
  if (isCenteredOverCell(monster)) {

  //2. Yes, it is, so find out which are valid directions to move.
  //`validDirections` returns an array which can include any
  //of these string values: "up", "right", "down", "left" or "none"
  monster.validDirections = validDirections(
    monster, wallMapArray, 0, world
  );

  //3. Can the monster change its direction?
  if (canChangeDirection(monster.validDirections)) {

    //4. If it can, choose the closest direction to the alien
    monster.direction = closestDirection(monster, alien, monster.validDirections);
  }
```

```
//5. Use the monster's direction and speed to find its new velocity
let velocity = directionToVelocity(monster.direction, monster.speed);
monster.vx = velocity.vx;
monster.vy = velocity.vy;
}
```

```
//6. Move the monster
monster.x += monster.vx;
monster.y += monster.vy;
```

The only new line of code is this one:

```
monster.direction = closestDirection(monster, alien, monster.validDirections);
```

A new function called closestDirection does the job of figuring out and returning one of the monster's valid directions that's closest to the alien. If there are no valid directions that match the closest direction, it falls back on selecting a random direction. Here's the complete closestDirection function that does all this:

```
function closestDirection(spriteOne, spriteTwo, validDirections = []) {

  //A helper function to find the closest direction
  let closest = () => {

    //Plot a vector between spriteTwo and spriteOne
    let vx = spriteTwo.centerX - spriteOne.centerX,
        vy = spriteTwo.centerY - spriteOne.centerY;

    //If the distance is greater on the X axis...
    if (Math.abs(vx) >= Math.abs(vy)) {

      //Try left and right
      if (vx <= 0) {
        return "left";
      } else {
        return "right";
      }
    }

    //If the distance is greater on the Y axis...
    else {

      //Try up and down
      if (vy <= 0) {
        return "up"
      } else {
        return "down"
      }
    }
  };
```

```
//The closest direction that's also a valid direction
let closestValidDirection = validDirections.find(x => x === closest());

//The `randomInt` helper function returns a random
//integer between a minimum and maximum value
let randomInt = (min, max) => {
  return Math.floor(Math.random() * (max - min + 1)) + min;
};

//Is the sprite trapped?
let trapped = validDirections.length === 0;

//If the sprite isn't trapped, choose the closest direction
//from the `validDirections` array. If there's no closest valid
//direction, then choose a valid direction at random
if (!trapped) {
  if (closestValidDirection) {
    return closestValidDirection;
  } else {
    return validDirections[randomInt(0, validDirections.length - 1)];
  }
} else {
  return "trapped"
  }
}
```

This function works by first plotting a vector between the two sprites, and then figuring out which direction would be the closest for spriteOne, the hunter, to reach spriteTwo, the target. The code checks whether that direction is also in the validDirections array. If it is, that closest direction is chosen, but if it isn't, a new random direction is chosen.

This system works well but there's a small problem with it: the monsters know which direction is the closest to the alien even if their sight is blocked by maze walls. Maybe the monsters are using sound to detect the alien's position, communicating telepathically, or, unlikely, they're just really smart? Aesthetically this system works – it looks correct and makes for a challenging game. But you might want to create a game where the monsters will only react if they can actually *see* the alien, unobstructed by walls. We can implement this feature by using an essential game design technique called **line of sight**.

Line of Sight

How can you tell whether a sprite can see another sprite? Plot a vector between two sprites and then check for obstructions at evenly spaced points along that vector. If the vector is completely unobstructed, then you know you have a direct line of sight between two sprites.

Run the lineOfSight.html file in this chapter's source files for an interactive example, shown in Figure 5-10. Drag and drop the alien, monster, and wall sprites in various combinations around the screen. A red line extends between the monster and the alien, which represents the line of sight. If the line of sight is unobstructed, the line between the sprites darkens and the monster opens its mouth.

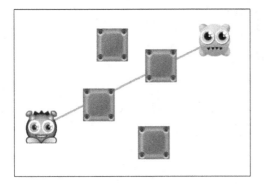 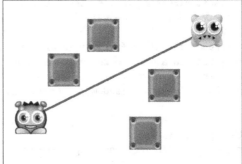

Figure 5-10. *Check for a line of sight between two sprites*

The way this works is that a series of points are invisibly placed along the vector (the line) between the two sprites. If any of those points touches a box, then you know that the line of sight is being obstructed. If none of those points touch any of the boxes, then there's a clear line of sight between the sprites. Figure 5-11 illustrates this.

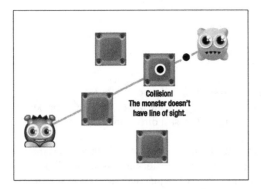 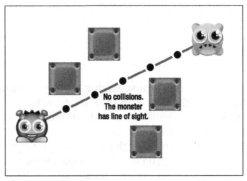

Figure 5-11. *Plot points along the line and check each point for a collision with a box*

Let's go a on step-by-step tour of the code you need to write to make this work.

Calculating the Vector

The first step is to plot a vector between the center of the two sprites.

```
let vx = spriteTwo.centerX - spriteOne.centerX,
    vy = spriteTwo.centerY - spriteOne.centerY;
```

Next, we need to find out what the length of the vector is, in pixels. The length of a vector is known as its **magnitude**, and you can figure it out like this:

```
let magnitude = Math.sqrt(vx * vx + vy * vy);
```

We want to plot points at evenly spaced positions along this vector. To help us do that, let's create a variable called segment that determines what the distance between each of those points should be.

```
let segment = spriteOne.width;
```

Usually you don't want the space between the points to be less than the width or height of your smallest sprite. That's because if the space between points is too large, the point collision test might skip over and miss smaller obstacle sprites.

Now that we know the length of the vector between the sprites, and we know the length of each segment between collision points, we can figure out how many collision points along the line we'll need to use.

```
let numberOfPoints = magnitude / segment;
```

For example, if the magnitude of the the vector is 256 pixels, and the length of each segment is 64 pixels, the numberOfPoints would be 4.

Finding the Positions of the Collision Points

We now have enough information to figure out the x/y position of the collision points along the vector. We're going to do this with the help of a function called points that returns an array containing objects with x and y properties. We're going to be able to use that array of point objects to test for a collision between between each point and an obstacle. Here's the point function that creates the array of point objects:

```
let points = () => {

  //Initialize an array that is going to store all our points
  //along the vector
  let arrayOfPoints = [];

  //Create a point object for each segment of the vector and
  //store its x/y position as well as its index number on
  //the map array
  for (let i = 1; i <= numberOfPoints; i++) {

    //Calculate the new magnitude for this iteration of the loop
    let newMagnitude = segment * i;

    //Find the unit vector
    let dx = vx / magnitude,
        dy = vy / magnitude;

    //Use the unit vector and newMagnitude to figure out the x/y
    //position of the next point in this loop iteration
    let x = spriteOne.centerX + dx * newMagnitude,
        y = spriteOne.centerY + dy * newMagnitude;

    //Push a point object with x and y properties into the `arrayOfPoints`
    arrayOfPoints.push({x, y});
  }
```

```
//Return the array of point objects
  return arrayOfPoints;
};
```

At the heart of the points function is a loop that creates point objects for however many numberOfPoints there are. The first thing the loop does is create a newMagnitude value by multiplying the loop index value with the value of segment.

```
let newMagnitude = segment * i;
```

If there are four points, and the width of each segment is 64 pixels, newMagnitude will have the values 64, 128, 194, and 256 with each iteration of the loop.

The next two lines of code figure out what the **unit vector** is, represented by the variable names dx and dy.

```
let dx = vx / magnitude,
    dy = vy / magnitude;
```

A unit vector (also known as a **normalized vector**) is just a tiny, scaled-down version of the main vector between the sprites that's less than one pixel long. It points in the same direction as the main vector, but because it's the smallest possible size that the vector can be, we can use it to create new vectors of varying length.

You'll find a complete beginner's guide to vector math in this book's companion, *Advanced Game Design with HTML5 and JavaScript* (Apress, 2015). It explains all these concepts in great detail with plenty of practical examples of how to use them for game development.

Multiplying the unit vector by the newMagnitude, and adding the result to spriteOne's position will give us the x/y positions of points along the vector.

```
let x = spriteOne.centerX + dx * newMagnitude,
    y = spriteOne.centerY + dy * newMagnitude;
```

Figure 5-12 illustrates what this would look like for each iteration of the loop if there were four numberOfPoints and the segment width was 64 pixels.

First point

Second point

Third point

Fourth point

Figure 5-12. *Find the positions of each of the points along the vector*

The x/y values of these points are stored in a point object and pushed into an array called `arrayOfPoints`.

```
arrayOfPoints.push({x, y});
```

When the loop finishes, `arrayOfPoints` will contain a list of objects with x and y properties that match the x and y values we calculated in the previous step. The `points` function returns this array:

```
return arrayOfPoints;
```

We can now access this array by calling the `points` function like this:

```
points()
```

This will dynamically recalculate and return the new array of points whenever we need them in our game.

Testing the Points for Collisions with Obstacles

We now need some way to figure out if any of those points is touching one of the obstacles. We can use a basic geometric collision function called `hitTestPoint` that checks whether a single point object with x/y properties is intersecting a rectangular sprite. `hitTestPoint` returns `true` if there is a collision, and `false` if there isn't.

```
let hitTestPoint = (point, sprite) => {

  //Find out if the point's position is inside the area defined
  //by the sprite's left, right, top and bottom sides
  let left = point.x > sprite.x,
      right = point.x < (sprite.x + sprite.width),
      top = point.y > sprite.y,
      bottom = point.y < (sprite.y + sprite.height);

  //If all the collision conditions are met, you know the
  //point is intersecting the sprite
  return left && right && top && bottom;
};
```

We can now use `hitTestPoint` to check for a collision between every point and every obstacle sprite that might be blocking the line of sight. Here's how:

```
let noObstacles = points().every(point => {
  return obstacles.every(obstacle => {
    return !(hitTestPoint(point, obstacle))
  });
});
```

If `noObstacles` is `true`, then we know that the line of sight is clear.

The lineOfSight Function

Let's put together all the techniques we've learned in the last few sections, and build a reusable `lineOfSight` function that will return `true` if there's a clear line of sight between two sprites, and `false` if there isn't. Here's how you'll be able to use it in your game code:

```
monster.lineOfSight = lineOfSight(
  monster, //Sprite one
  alien,   //Sprite two
  boxes,   //An array of obstacle sprites
  16       //The distance between each collision point
);
```

The fourth argument determines the distance between collision points. For better performance, make this a large number, up to the maximum width of your smallest sprite (such as 64 or 32). For greater precision, use a smaller number.

You can use the `lineOfSight` value to decide how to change certain things in your game. In the lineOfSight.html example file, it's used to open the monster's mouth, and to increase the `alpha` value of the connecting line between the two sprites.

```
if (monster.lineOfSight) {
  monster.show(monster.states.angry)
  line.alpha = 1;
} else {
  monster.show(monster.states.normal)
  line.alpha = 0.3;
}
```

(Check out the source code in the lineOfSight.js file for full details on how this works, and especially how to initialize the monster's different states.)

Here's the complete `lineOfSight` function.

```
function lineOfSight(
  spriteOne,     //The first sprite, with `centerX` and `centerY` properties
  spriteTwo,     //The second sprite, with `centerX` and `centerY` properties
  obstacles,     //An array of sprites which act as obstacles
  segment = 32   //The distance between collision points
) {

  //Plot a vector between spriteTwo and spriteOne
  let vx = spriteTwo.centerX - spriteOne.centerX,
      vy = spriteTwo.centerY - spriteOne.centerY;

  //Find the vector's magnitude (its length in pixels)
  let magnitude = Math.sqrt(vx * vx + vy * vy);

  //How many points will we need to test?
  let numberOfPoints = magnitude / segment;
```

```
//Create an array of x/y points, separated by 64 pixels, that
//extends from `spriteOne` to `spriteTwo`
let points = () => {

  //Initialize an array that is going to store all our points
  //along the vector
  let arrayOfPoints = [];

  //Create a point object for each segment of the vector and
  //store its x/y position as well as its index number on
  //the map array
  for (let i = 1; i <= numberOfPoints; i++) {

    //Calculate the new magnitude for this iteration of the loop
    let newMagnitude = segment * i;

    //Find the unit vector
    let dx = vx / magnitude,
        dy = vy / magnitude;

    //Use the unit vector and newMagnitude to figure out the x/y
    //position of the next point in this loop iteration
    let x = spriteOne.centerX + dx * newMagnitude,
        y = spriteOne.centerY + dy * newMagnitude;

    //Push a point object with x and y properties into the `arrayOfPoints`
    arrayOfPoints.push({x, y});
  }

  //Return the array of point objects
  return arrayOfPoints;
};

//Test for a collision between a point and a sprite
let hitTestPoint = (point, sprite) => {

  //Find out if the point's position is inside the area defined
  //by the sprite's left, right, top and bottom sides
  let left = point.x > sprite.x,
      right = point.x < (sprite.x + sprite.width),
      top = point.y > sprite.y,
      bottom = point.y < (sprite.y + sprite.height);

  //If all the collision conditions are met, you know the
  //point is intersecting the sprite
  return left && right && top && bottom;
};

//The `noObstacles` function will return `true` if all the tile
//index numbers along the vector are `0`, which means they contain
```

```
//no obstacles. If any of them aren't `0`, then the function returns
//`false` which means there's an obstacle in the way
let noObstacles = points().every(point => {
  return obstacles.every(obstacle => {
    return !(hitTestPoint(point, obstacle))
  });
});

//Return the true/false value of the collision test
return noObstacles;
}
```

So now you know how to figure out if there's a clear line of sight between two sprites. And, you also know how to make sprites navigate around a maze environment. The last thing you need to learn is how to combine these two techniques – don't worry, it's much easier than you think!

Tile-Based Line of Sight

Run the tileBasedLineOfSight.html file in the chapter's source files for a working example of how to implement a line of sight pathfinding system in a tile-based maze environment. In this example the monsters only chase the alien if they have a clear line of sight down a passage, as illustrated in Figure 5-13.

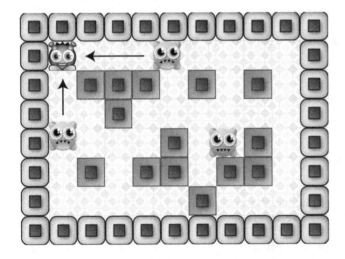

Figure 5-13. *The monsters only chase the alien when they can see it*

There are two modifications we're going to make our line of sight system so that it works well in a tile-based maze environment:

- We're going to use a tile-based collision instead of a geometry-based collision to check whether any of the points along the vector between the sprites are touching any walls.

- We're going to restrict the vector between the sprites to right angles. That means we're only going to allow angles of 0, 90, or 180 degrees to test for a line of sight.

Let's find out how to add these two new features and then use them to build a new `tileBaseLineOfSight` function.

Tile-Based Collision

The advantage to using a tile-based collision system in a maze game environment is that it's very efficient. In a big game you could have hundreds of tile-based collision tests happening simultaneously without any noticeable performance hit. Geometry-based collision is much more math heavy, so; although it can be very precise, you pay a performance penalty.

In our earlier line of sight example we used a geometry based collision function called `hitTestPoint` that checked whether a point is inside the area of a rectangle. How can we test for a collision between a point and a sprite using tile based collision? We need to test whether a point's map array index number corresponds to the map array index number of the sprite we want to test for a collision with. That means that we need to convert each point's x/y position number into a map array index number. We already know how to do that, using a function called `getIndex` that you learned to use in Chapter 3:

```
function getIndex(x, y, tilewidth, tileheight, mapWidthInTiles) {

  //Convert pixel coordinates to map index coordinates
  let index = {};
  index.x = Math.floor(x / tilewidth);
  index.y = Math.floor(y / tileheight);

  //Return the index number
  return index.x + (index.y * mapWidthInTiles);
};
```

If you have an array of points, all of which have index numbers that correspond to their positions on the map, you know that they're colliding with any objects that share those same index numbers. You can then find out exactly what object the point is colliding with by using the point's index number to look up the `gid` value of the cell at the location.

```
mapArray[point.index]
```

If the point's `gid` number matches the `gid` number of an object that you're interested in, then you have a collision.

For a line of sight collision test, you're specifically looking for collisions with cells that *don't contain any obstacles*. In the examples we've been using in this book, all empty cells without obstacles have `gid` numbers of 0. That means you can loop through every point in the line of sight vector, and if all of them have index numbers that correspond to a `gid` value of 0, then you know there are no collisions.

```
let noObstacles = points().every(point => {
  return mapArray[point.index] === 0
});
```

In the example above, if `noObstacles` returns `true`, then you have a clear line of sight. You'll see ahead how this little bit of code is used in our complete tile-based collision system. But first, how can we limit our line of sight test to allow only right angles?

Limiting the Angle

In our earlier line of sight example the monster sprite had a full field of 360 degree vision. In the maze game example, the monsters' line of sight is restricted to right angles. This means that the the monsters can't see around corners on the diagonal; they can just see whatever is directly in front of them. This makes it a little bit easier for the player, and also makes for a more natural feeling maze game experience.

Before we find out how to implement this, let's first find our how you can figure out the angle of a vector (a line). As you've learned, a vector is defined by two values: vx and vy. This is the code that we've been using to plot a vector between two sprites:

```
let vx = spriteTwo.centerX - spriteOne.centerX,
    vy = spriteTwo.centerY - spriteOne.centerY;
```

You can find out what the angle of that vector is, in degrees, using this handy formula:

```
let angle = Math.atan2(vy, vx) * 180 / Math.PI;
```

The first step in restricting the line of sight angle is to create an array that includes all the valid angles. For example, to restrict your angles to 90 degrees, use these angles:

```
let angles = [90, -90, 0, 180, -180];
```

The next step is to create a function that compares the vector's angle to the angles in the array. If they match, the function returns true, if they don't, it returns false. Here's a validAngle function that does this:

```
let validAngle = (vx, vy, angles) => {

  //Find the angle of the vector between the two sprites
  let angle = Math.atan2(vy, vx) * 180 / Math.PI;

  //If the angle matches one of the valid angles, return
  //`true`, otherwise return `false`
  if (angles.length !== 0) {
    return angles.some(x => x === angle);
  } else {
    return true;
  }
};
```

Now let's find out how to use these new techniques to build a reusable tile-based line of sight function.

The tileBasedLineOfSight Function

Here's the new tileBasedLineOfSight function that implements tile-based collision and restricts the angle to 90 degrees. You'll learn ahead how to use it in a game.

```
function tileBasedLineOfSight(
  spriteOne,    //The first sprite, with `centerX` and `centerY` properties
  spriteTwo,    //The second sprite, with `centerX` and `centerY` properties
  mapArray,     //The tile map array
```

```
  world,          //The `world` object that contains the `tilewidth
                  //`tileheight` and `widthInTiles` properties
  emptyGid = 0,   //The Gid that represents and empty tile, usually `0`
  segment = 32,   //The distance between collision points
  angles = []     //An array of angles to which you want to
                  //restrict the line of sight
) {

  //Plot a vector between spriteTwo and spriteOne
  let vx = spriteTwo.centerX - spriteOne.centerX,
      vy = spriteTwo.centerY - spriteOne.centerY;


  //Find the vector's magnitude (its length in pixels)
  let magnitude = Math.sqrt(vx * vx + vy * vy);


  //How many points will we need to test?
  let numberOfPoints = magnitude / segment;


  //Create an array of x/y points that
  //extends from `spriteOne` to `spriteTwo`
  let points = () => {

    //Initialize an array that is going to store all our points
    //along the vector
    let arrayOfPoints = [];

    //Create a point object for each segment of the vector and
    //store its x/y position as well as its index number on
    //the map array
    for (let i = 1; i <= numberOfPoints; i++) {

      //Calculate the new magnitude for this iteration of the loop
      let newMagnitude = segment * i;

      //Find the unit vector
      let dx = vx / magnitude,
          dy = vy / magnitude;

      //Use the unit vector and newMagnitude to figure out the x/y
      //position of the next point in this loop iteration
      let x = spriteOne.centerX + dx * newMagnitude,
          y = spriteOne.centerY + dy * newMagnitude;

      //The getIndex function converts x/y coordinates into
      //map array index positon numbers
      let getIndex = (x, y, tilewidth, tileheight, mapWidthInTiles) => {

        //Convert pixel coordinates to map index coordinates
        let index = {};
        index.x = Math.floor(x / tilewidth);
        index.y = Math.floor(y / tileheight);
```

```
    //Return the index number
    return index.x + (index.y * mapWidthInTiles);
  };

  //Find the map index number that this x and y point corresponds to
  let index = getIndex(
    x, y,
    world.tilewidth,
    world.tileheight,
    world.widthInTiles
  );

  //Push the point into the `arrayOfPoints`
  arrayOfPoints.push({
    x, y, index
  });
  }


  //Return the array
  return arrayOfPoints;
};

//The tile-based collision test.
//The `noObstacles` function will return `true` if all the tile
//index numbers along the vector are `0`, which means they contain
//no walls. If any of them aren't 0, then the function returns
//`false` which means there's a wall in the way
let noObstacles = points().every(point => {
    return mapArray[point.index] === emptyGid
});

//Restrict the line of sight to right angles only
//(we don't want to use diagonals)
let validAngle = () => {

  //Find the angle of the vector between the two sprites
  let angle = Math.atan2(vy, vx) * 180 / Math.PI;

  //If the angle matches one of the valid angles, return
  //`true`, otherwise return `false`
  if (angles.length !== 0) {
    return angles.some(x => x === angle);
  } else {
    return true;
  }
};
```

```
//Return `true` if there are no obstacles and the line of sight
//is at a 90 degree angle
if (noObstacles === true && validAngle() === true) {
  return true;
} else {
  return false;
}
}
```

And that's tile-based line of sight - solved!

Summary

All the basics you need to know to get started with pathfinding are in this chapter. You've learned how to analyze and interpret the environment that a sprite is in, and how to use that information to decide which direction a sprite should move in. Should it choose a random direction, or a direction that's closest to its target? You've also learned one of the most important techniques that every game developer needs to know: how to determine the line of sight. And, you now know how to use a line of sight in both a geometry-based and a tile-based collision environment. As you'll see in the chapters ahead, all these skills are useful not just for pathfinding, but also as the basis for building rudimentary AIs. And, of course, you can use these exact same techniques with your isometric game maps!

The skills you've learned in this chapter will take you quite far, but there's one more important pathfinding skill you need to know: how to find the the shortest path between two points. That's what the next chapter is all about!

CHAPTER 6

■ ■ ■

Finding the Shortest Path

There is one last major area of pathfinding we need to tackle: finding the shortest path through a maze. As it turns out, this is not just an interesting aside, but one of the most important game design skills you need to know.

All the player control systems that we've covered in the book so far have involved moving the player around the screen with the keyboard or the mouse. But games often employ a point-and-click control system. Point the mouse to some place on the map and click. The character will walk there and magically seem to find the shortest path to the destination while cleverly sidestepping any obstacles. Graphical adventure games use this control system, as do almost all strategy and turn-based games. How does it work? That's exactly what you're going to find out in this chapter!

Moving a character along the shortest path is really a two-part process:

1. Find the shortest path: This involves testing all the most likely tiles between the start point and the destination. You need to figure out which tiles will get you to the destination sooner, and which contain obstacles to avoid. At the end of this testing, you end up with an array of tiles that tell you the shortest path.

2. Follow the tiles in the path: The arrays of tiles you end up with are like breadcrumbs that the game character can follow. Tell the character to follow these crumbs from its start position to the destination.

If the first step seems like it might be rather complex, it is! But the good news is that excellent solutions have been found already. That means you don't need to worry about coming up with your own solution — you can just choose a ready-made one and implement it in your game.

There are a number of different pathfinding algorithms you can use, including best-first, breadth- first, and Dijkstra's algorithm. All will do a reasonable job of solving the problem. But the best is generally regarded to be A* (A star). The A* algorithm has the overall best performance, and it is extremely flexible. If there's only one pathfinding algorithm you should learn, A* is it.

A* was developed in the 1960s by Peter Hart, Nils Nilsson, and Bertram Raphael. It's a modification to Dijkstra's algorithm, a pathfinding algorithm that was postulated in the 1950s by pioneering computer scientist Edsger Dijkstra.

Before I show you how to use A* in a game, let's take a detailed look at how the algorithm works.

© Rex van der Spuy 2017
R. van der Spuy, *The Advanced Game Developer's Toolkit*, DOI 10.1007/978-1-4842-1097-0_6

Understanding A*

We can be proud of our evolutionary ancestors. Thanks to good pathfinding ability, they all successfully evaded larger protozoa, sidestepped gnashing dinosaur teeth, and avoided ending up as fossilized remains at the bottom of the Sterkfontein caves. Pathfinding is a skill that is as essential to being able to survive as a tree frog in the Amazon as it is to being able to catch the bus in the morning. It's a survival skill that allows you to automatically figure out the shortest path from point A to point B without being eaten, dying of starvation, or being late for work. One glance at Figure 6-1, and you'll immediately be able to see the shortest path between point A and point B. Pathfinding is part of our DNA.

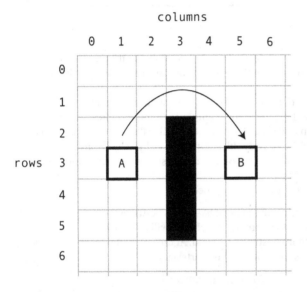

Figure 6-1. *What's the shortest path between point A and point B? It's obvious to us humans, but how do you explain it to a computer?*

Computers, on the other hand, are like pampered, prize-winning, Persian lap cats. They sit around all day, spend far too much time on the Internet, and sleep a lot. They haven't had their skills honed through countless millennia of fighting it out in the primordial soup as we have. We need to tell them in the bluntest growl possible, "This path good!" or "This path not good!" and practically threaten them with a gnarled club.

But what is a "good path"? In the case of finding the shortest path, it's the one that gets you to your destination sooner. The problem is that computers can't see the big picture. They can see only one small step at a time. So the strategy for telling a computer how to find the shortest path goes something like this:

- Break the entire path into many small steps.

- For each step, figure out which step to take next.

- Take that next step, and repeat the process until you get where you're supposed to be.

But the computer must still be able to tell the difference between a good path and a bad path. Let's see how to help it figure that out.

Calculating Costs

Solve this riddle:

A newspaper is delivered to your front door every morning. What's the least expensive way of picking it up?

A. Opening the front door.

B. Walking out the back door, jumping over your garden fence, running down the alley, hailing a taxicab, and riding around the block to your front door?

Option A was free, but option B cost you about $4.75 in cab fare. This means that option B is more **expensive**.

Expensive is the term that the A* algorithm uses to describe how much work it takes to travel between two points. A* figures out the least expensive routes to a destination. It does this by assigning a cost to every possible step you can take on the path. The step with the lowest cost is the better step to take. A* works by finding the lowest cost moves and the least expensive paths.

A* has its own set of terms and vocabulary. Cost and expense are two of those terms and, as you'll see, they're a convenient way to describe some of its core concepts. I'll be introducing a few other specific A* terms ahead. Keep a special lookout for the terms "node" and "heuristic," coming up soon!

Figure 6-2 explains what I mean by cost. Imagine that you're a bacterium in a Petri dish, free floating, and minding your own business at point A. Suddenly, the shadow of a huge, hungry single-celled amoeba looms over you with the lone goal of subsuming your cellular matter. You know you're in trouble if you don't hide right away. There are only two places you can hide: point B or point C. You have a split second to decide which is the closest.

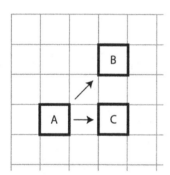

Figure 6-2. *Which is closest to A: B or C?*

In the example in Figure 6-2, traveling to point B takes about one-third longer than traveling to point C. In fact, it takes exactly 1.41 times longer to travel to point B from point A. That means that point C is where you need to swim to escape that amoeba. The value 1.41 is the cost of traveling diagonally.

In a rectangular grid-based game world, there are only two choices of movement, and each has a cost:

- **Diagonally**: The cost is 14.

- **Directly across**: Going horizontally or vertically, the cost is 10.

It doesn't really matter what those costs are, as long as they proportionately represent the amount of time it takes to move in those directions. So, 14 versus 10 is the same proportion as 1.4 versus 1, and we conveniently don't need to worry about decimal numbers. You can certainly use 1.4 and 1 in your own code if you prefer. Figure 6-3 shows the cost of movement between cells.

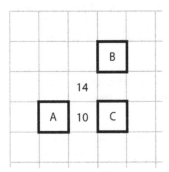

Figure 6-3. *The cost of traveling through cells*

Now we have a way of describing to the computer what a good path is: the one with the lowest cost.

Figure 6-4 shows two possible paths from A to B. Not only can you clearly see that path 1 is the shortest, but it also happens to be the least expensive.

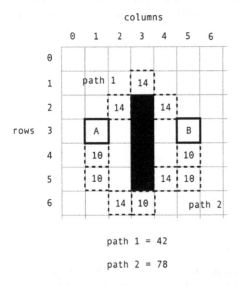

Figure 6-4. *The shortest path is also the least expensive*

Earlier, I mentioned that computers can see only one step in the path at any given time. You can see from Figure 6-3 that each step is the least expensive step that could have been chosen to get to point B. But that's only obvious after you already know the outcome of the path. The computer doesn't know this before it starts building the path. How does it know which step to take next, directly from point A?

Finding the Second Step

In A*'s terminology, every step in the path is called a node. As far as we're concerned, nodes are just cells in a two-dimensional array or grid. However, I'm going to start calling them nodes from now on, just so that you get used to that term. You'll find it widely used in discussions of pathfinding in other texts. A* uses the term node because there's no reason why you can't divide your space in ways other than a rectangular grid, such as by using hexagons or circles. But for our purposes, when you hear me talk about nodes, just know that I mean grid cells.

A* starts searching for the shortest path at point A. Point A is the parent node. A parent node is a definite, confirmed step on the path. Obviously, we know that point A is going to be the first step, so it automatically becomes the first parent node.

If we know what the first step is, how do we find the second step? A* must check all eight cells surrounding the parent node to discover which of those is the next most likely candidate. Figure 6-5 shows point A as the parent node, and all the surrounding nodes that it needs to check. (If any of those nodes happen to be walls or impassable objects, it ignores them.)

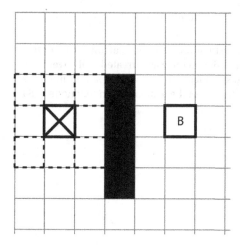

Figure 6-5. *Check all the nodes surrounding the parent to see which might be the next most likely step in the path*

Each of these surrounding cells declares the current parent node as its parent. The code that does this in the A* algorithm will look something like this:

```
surroundingNode.parent = currentParent;
```

This is important because it means that A* can trace the best path to the destination by following the trail of parent nodes. Don't worry too much about this now, as you'll see how it works in the pages ahead. Just remember that each node has a `parent` property that keeps track of the node that it's linked to in the path.

A* then needs to find out what the cost will be to travel from the parent node to the surrounding child nodes. It turns out that this happens to be an important number, so A* refers to this cost as G. Figure 6-6 shows the G costs for all the surrounding nodes.

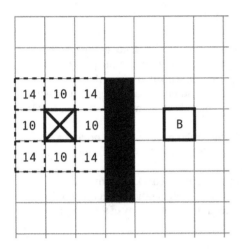

Figure 6-6. *Each surrounding node is given a cost, referred to in A*'s terminology as G*

A* then figures out which surrounding node is closer to the destination, point B. It calculates the cost of traveling from point B to every surrounding node. (The wall standing in the way is treated as if it were not there for now, but as you'll see, this is compensated for by later tests.) Figure 6-7 shows the path from the first surrounding node to point B. You can see that it calculated the cost of the test path from that node as 54.

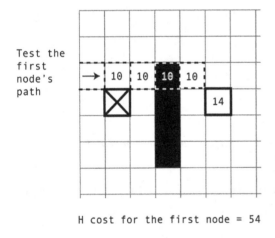

Figure 6-7. *Figure out the cost of each path from every surrounding node to point B*

This distance test is called a heuristic. Heuristic simply means figuring something out by trial and error. (It's derived from the Greek work *heuriskein*, which means find.) Heuristic is not random trial and error, however. It's trial and error within a set of logical rules that are likely to produce the answer we're seeking. A* has no idea which of the surrounding child nodes will end up with the least expensive path, so it just tries all eight of them. The cost of each heuristic path also happens to be very important, so A* refers to this cost as **H**.

There are actually three commonly used ways of calculating the heuristic path: Manhattan, Euclidean, and diagonal. We'll be looking at each of these in detail in the "Understanding Heuristics" section later in this chapter. For now, just know that these are specific ways for calculating the distance from the surrounding test node to the destination point.

A* figures out the H cost for every surrounding child node. If you combine the H and G costs, you come up with a third, final cost, called F. Figure 6-8 shows what all the G, H, and F costs are for each node.

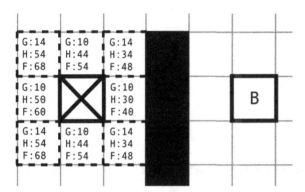

Figure 6-8. *Find the final F cost of each node by adding the G and H costs together*

The winner is the node with the lowest F cost. Can you see it? It's the one directly to the right of the parent node, as shown in Figure 6-9.

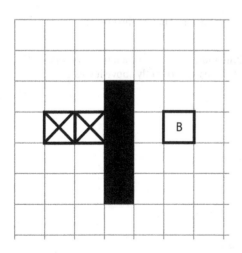

Figure 6-9. *The node with the lowest F cost becomes the most likely next step in the path*

This node now becomes a potential new parent node. A* doesn't yet know for sure whether this will be the best second step to take, but as far as it can tell, it's a pretty good place to continue checking. (In fact, it's not the best second step, but A* will soon find this out, as you will see.)

You can see from Figure 6-9 that each parent node represents a potential step in the path to point B. I use the word *potential* because A* doesn't know for sure whether any given parent node is the best step until it does a little more checking. You can already see a problem occurring in Figure 6-9. The new parent node is *not* the best next step. It would be better to move diagonally up from point A. Figure 6-10 illustrates this.

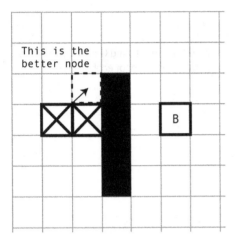

Figure 6-10. *The obvious first choice isn't always the best one. How will A* figure out that it's better to move diagonally up from the start point?*

Luckily, A* has a system for cross-checking nodes and weeding out inefficiencies like this. A* keeps track of the possible best parent nodes to use for the route by keeping two lists:

- Closed list: This is a list of nodes that don't need to be checked. Whenever a new parent node is found, it's added to this list.

- Open list: This is a list of all the nodes surrounding each parent. They're the nodes that need to be checked.

When a new potential parent node checks all the surrounding nodes, it looks at each node's previous G cost on the open list. Figure 6-11 shows that the previous G cost for the node directly above it was 14.

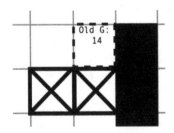

Figure 6-11. *The old G cost was 14. Will its new cost be more or less?*

To find its new G cost, A* takes the current G value of the parent node and adds 10 more, which is the cost of traveling up one node. That brings the total new G cost to 20. Figure 6-12 illustrates this.

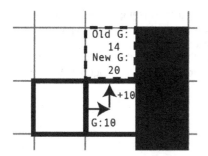

Figure 6-12. *Add the parent node's G cost (10) to the cost of traveling up one node (10) to find the new G cost (20)*

If it finds that the new cost is lower, A* changes the node's parent to the current parent:

```
if (newG < oldG) {
  surroundingNode.parent = currentParent;
} else {
  don't change the surrounding node's parent
}
```

But if the new G cost is more expensive, the node's parent doesn't change. That's the case in this example. It will keep the same parent that it was assigned in the first step, which was the start node. The current parent node that we're checking is left out in the cold.

This is very important because A* creates the path by linking nodes together through their parents, like a chain.

A* runs this same check with all the other surrounding nodes, and calculates their new G costs based on what they will be if they need to run through the new parent, as shown in Figure 6-13.

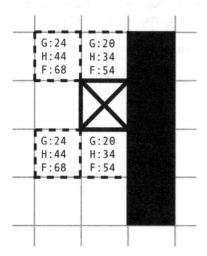

Figure 6-13. *Find out if any of the G costs of the other nodes are less by routing the path through this current parent. They're not*

As you can see from Figure 6-13, the G costs of all the nodes will be higher by going through the current parent. That means that none of them will change their parent to the current parent. The current parent is toast! It has no children, so it's definitely not going to be part of the shortest path.

But A* still needs to figure out which node to test next. It ignores wall nodes and the previous parent node. It chooses the next node with the lowest F cost as the new parent node, as shown in Figure 6-14.

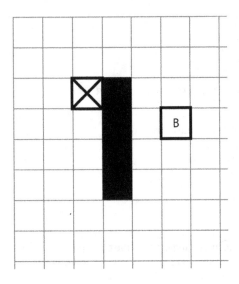

Figure 6-14. *The surrounding node with the lowest F cost becomes the new parent node*

But what happens if some of the nodes have the same cost? You can see from Figure 6-13 that the nodes directly above and below the parent are tied for first place, each with the same low score of 54. In this case, A* chooses whichever node comes up first in the loop that runs this check. If it happens to be the wrong one, this will be corrected later by further checks. But by pure chance, this time the first node with the lowest score also happens to be the better choice. It's chosen as the new parent node, and A* continues checking.

It's also quite likely that there will be more than one possible shortest path. The one A* builds is determined by how it selects nodes whose costs are tied.

We've currently tested two nodes, and have selected a third, as you can see from Figure 6-15.

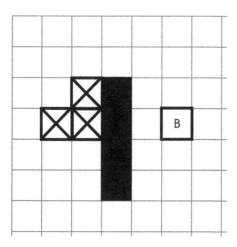

Figure 6-15. *Three nodes are candidates for steps on the path, but which will make the final shakedown?*

But only two of those nodes are part of the path. How do we know? Because the node on the upper right has assigned the start node as its parent. This is a relationship that chains the two nodes together, as shown in Figure 6-16. It forms the first two steps in the path.

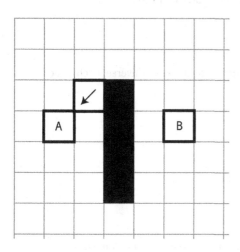

Figure 6-16. *The start node is the parent of the upper-right node. This relationship chains the nodes together*

Linking the Nodes Through Their Parents

A* then continues following this same logic until it reaches the destination node, point B. In a very big game world, this could involve checking hundreds of nodes.

When A* finally builds the path, it traces the route from parent node to parent node to link the start and end points together. You can see this illustrated in Figure 6-17.

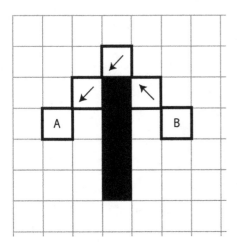

Figure 6-17. Each node in the final path has a reference to its parent

When A* reaches the destination, point B, it stops checking. A* then just needs to work backward from point B, following the parent nodes, to construct the path. The A* algorithm produces an array that will tell you each node you need to walk through to find the shortest route from point A to point B.

Now that you understand the theory, let's have a look at the actual JavaScript code.

A* in Code

It should be pretty obvious by now that nodes are quite important things in the A* universe. Each node needs to store quite a bit of information:

- Its position (its row and column on the grid).
- Its G, H, and F costs.
- Its parent node.

It therefore makes sense to create a node object to store this information.

Creating a Node Map

The first step to working with nodes is to create something called a **node map**. The node map is a two-dimensional array that exactly matches the game's maze map. However, each cell of the node map contains a node object. These node objects will store all the important node properties and values we need.

Here's a simple function called nodes that returns an array of node objects for every cell in our map array.

```
let nodes = (mapArray, mapWidthInTiles) => {
  return mapArray.map((cell, index) => {

    //Figure out the row and column of this cell
    let column = index % mapWidthInTiles;
    let row = Math.floor(index / mapWidthInTiles);
```

```
//The node object
return node = {
    f: 0,
    g: 0,
    h: 0,
    parent: null,
    column: column,
    row: row,
    index: index
  };
});
};
```

Each node object includes cost properties, a reference to its parent node, and row column and index information that will make it each for us to match the node up its position in the map array. You'll see how this is used in the context of the shortestPath function that we're going to look at next.

The shortestPath Function

The heart of our A* code is the shortestPath function. It returns an array that contains the shortest path from point A to point B. Here's an example of how to call it, including the arguments to use.

```
let path = shortestPath(
  getIndex(alien.x, alien.y, 64, 64, 13),         //The start map index
  getIndex(g.pointer.x, g.pointer.y, 64, 64, 13)), //The destination index
  wallMapArray,                                    //The map array
  13,                                              //Map width, in tiles
  [2, 3],                                          //Obstacle gid array
  "manhattan"                                      //Heuristic to use
);
```

As you can see, the arguments match the kinds of information that we looked at earlier. The one thing we haven't discussed yet is the kind of heuristic to use. I'll explain the heuristic options and how they work in the "Understanding Heuristics" section.

The following is the entire shortestPath function. Apart from a few additional checks that it needs to make sure that all the data is valid, it's doing pathfinding just as I explained in the description of how the A* algorithm works. Read through all the comments and try to match up the code to the earlier description.

```
function shortestPath(
  startIndex,
  destinationIndex,
  mapArray,
  mapWidthInTiles,
  obstacleGids = [],
  heuristic = "manhattan"
) {

  //The `nodes` function creates the array of node objects
  let nodes = (mapArray, mapWidthInTiles) => {
    return mapArray.map((cell, index) => {
```

```
//Figure out the row and column of this cell
let column = index % mapWidthInTiles;
let row = Math.floor(index / mapWidthInTiles);

//The node object
return node = {
  f: 0,
  g: 0,
  h: 0,
  parent: null,
  column: column,
  row: row,
  index: index
  };
  });
};

//Initialize the shortestPath array
let shortestPath = [];

//Initialize the node map
let nodeMap = nodes(mapArray, mapWidthInTiles);

//Initialize the closed and open list arrays
let closedList = [];
let openList = [];

//Declare the "costs" of travelling in straight or diagonal lines
let straightCost = 10;
let diagonalCost = 14;

//Get the start node
let startNode = nodeMap[startIndex];

//Get the current center node. The first one will
//match the path's start position
let centerNode = startNode;

//Push the `centerNode` into the `openList`, because
//it's the first node that we're going to check
openList.push(centerNode)

//Get the current destination node. The first one will
//match the path's end position
let destinationNode = nodeMap[destinationIndex];

//All the nodes that are surrounding the current map index number
let surroundingNodes = (index, mapArray, mapWidthInTiles) => {

  //Find out what all the surrounding nodes are (including those that
  //might be beyond the borders of the map - we'll filter these out ahead
```

```
//in the `validSurroundingNodes` function)
let allSurroundingNodes = [
  nodeMap[index - mapWidthInTiles - 1],
  nodeMap[index - mapWidthInTiles],
  nodeMap[index - mapWidthInTiles + 1],
  nodeMap[index - 1],
  nodeMap[index + 1],
  nodeMap[index + mapWidthInTiles - 1],
  nodeMap[index + mapWidthInTiles],
  nodeMap[index + mapWidthInTiles + 1]
];


//Optionally exlude the diagonal nodes, which is often perferable
//for 2D maze games
let crossSurroundingNodes = [
  nodeMap[index - mapWidthInTiles],
  nodeMap[index - 1],
  nodeMap[index + 1],
  nodeMap[index + mapWidthInTiles],
];


//Find the valid sourrounding nodes, which are ones inside
//the map border that don't incldue obstacles. Optionally change `allSurroundingNodes`
//to `crossSurroundingNodes` to prevent the path from choosing diagonal routes
//between nodes
let validSurroundingNodes = allSurroundingNodes.filter(node => {

  //The node will be beyond the top and bottom edges of the
  //map if it is `undefined`
  let nodeIsWithinTopAndBottomBounds = node !== undefined;

  //Only return nodes that are within the top and bottom map bounds
  if (nodeIsWithinTopAndBottomBounds) {

    //Some Boolean values that tell us whether the current map index is on
    //the left or right border of the map, and whether any of the nodes
    //surrounding that index extend beyond the left and right borders
    let indexIsOnLeftBorder = index % mapWidthInTiles === 0
    let indexIsOnRightBorder = (index + 1) % mapWidthInTiles === 0
    let nodeIsBeyondLeftBorder
      = node.column % (mapWidthInTiles - 1) === 0
      && node.column !== 0;
    let nodeIsBeyondRightBorder = node.column % mapWidthInTiles === 0

    //Find out whether of not the node contains an obstacle by looping
    //through the obstacle gids and and returning `true` if it
    //finds any at this node's location
    let nodeContainsAnObstacle = obstacleGids.some(obstacle => {
      return mapArray[node.index] === obstacle;
    });
```

```
    //If the index is on the left border and any nodes surrounding it are beyond the
    //left border, don't return that node
    if (indexIsOnLeftBorder) {
      return !nodeIsBeyondLeftBorder;
    }

    //If the index is on the right border and any nodes surrounding it are beyond the
    //right border, don't return that node
    else if (indexIsOnRightBorder) {
      return !nodeIsBeyondRightBorder;
    }

    //Return `false` if the node contains an obstacle
    else if (nodeContainsAnObstacle) {
      return false;
    }

    //If this passes the checks above, it means the index must be
    //inside the area defined by the left and right borders.
    //So, return the node
    else {
      return true;
    }
  }
});


  //Return the array of `validSurroundingNodes`
  return validSurroundingNodes;
};


//Heuristic methods
//1. Manhattan
let manhattan = (testNode, destinationNode) => {
  let h
    = Math.abs(testNode.row - destinationNode.row)
    * straightCost + Math.abs(testNode.column - destinationNode.column)
    * straightCost;
  return h;
};


//2. Euclidean
let euclidean = (testNode, destinationNode) => {
  let vx = destinationNode.column - testNode.column,
    vy = destinationNode.row - testNode.row,
    h = Math.floor(Math.sqrt(vx * vx + vy * vy) * straightCost);
  return h;
};


//3. Diagonal
let diagonal = (testNode, destinationNode) => {
  let vx = Math.abs(destinationNode.column - testNode.column),
```

```
    vy = Math.abs(destinationNode.row - testNode.row),
    h = 0;

  if (vx > vy) {
    h = Math.floor(diagonalCost * vy + straightCost * (vx - vy));
  } else {
    h = Math.floor(diagonalCost * vx + straightCost * (vy - vx));
  }
  return h;
};
```

```
//Loop through all the nodes until the current `centerNode` matches the
//`destinationNode`. When they're the same we know we've reached the
//end of the path
while (centerNode !== destinationNode) {

  //Find all the nodes surrounding the current `centerNode`
  let surroundingTestNodes = surroundingNodes(centerNode.index, mapArray,
mapWidthInTiles);

  //Loop through all the `surroundingTestNodes` using a classic `for` loop
  //(A `for` loop gives us a marginal performance boost. A* is extremely performance
  //hungery, so even a small performance boost with each loop iteration can
  //amount to a significant boost overall)
  for (let i = 0; i < surroundingTestNodes.length; i++) {

    //Get a reference to the current test node
    let testNode = surroundingTestNodes[i];

    //Find out whether the node is on a straight axis or
    //a diagonal axis, and assign the appropriate cost

    //A. Declare the cost variable
    let cost = 0;

    //B. Do they occupy the same row or column?
    if (centerNode.row === testNode.row || centerNode.column === testNode.column) {

      //If they do, assign a cost of "10"
      cost = straightCost;
    } else {

      //Otherwise, assign a cost of "14"
      cost = diagonalCost;
    }

    //C. Calculate the costs (g, h and f)
    //The node's current cost
    let g = centerNode.g + cost;

    //The cost of travelling from this node to the
    //destination node (the heuristic)
```

147

```
let h;
switch (heuristic) {
  case "manhattan":
    h = manhattan(testNode, destinationNode);
    break;

  case "euclidean":
    h = euclidean(testNode, destinationNode);
    break;

  case "diagonal":
    h = diagonal(testNode, destinationNode);
    break;

  default:
    throw new Error("Oops! It looks like you misspelled the name of the heuristic");
}

//The final cost
let f = g + h;

//Find out if the testNode is in either
//the openList or closedList array
let isOnOpenList = openList.some(node => testNode === node);
let isOnClosedList = closedList.some(node => testNode === node);

//If it's on either of these lists, we can check
//whether this route is a lower-cost alternative
//to the previous cost calculation. The new G cost
//will make the difference to the final F cost
if (isOnOpenList || isOnClosedList) {
  if (testNode.f > f) {
    testNode.f = f;
    testNode.g = g;
    testNode.h = h;

    //Only change the parent if the new cost is lower
    testNode.parent = centerNode;
  }
}

//Otherwise, add the testNode to the open list
else {
  testNode.f = f;
  testNode.g = g;
  testNode.h = h;
  testNode.parent = centerNode;
  openList.push(testNode);
}
```

```
    //The `for` loop ends here
    }

    //Push the current centerNode into the closed list
    closedList.push(centerNode);

    //Quit the loop if there's nothing on the open list.
    //This means that there is no path to the destination or the
    //destination is invalid, like a wall tile
    if (openList.length === 0) {
      return shortestPath;
    }

    //Sort the open list according to final cost
    openList = openList.sort((a, b) => a.f - b.f);

    //Set the node with the lowest final cost as the new centerNode
    centerNode = openList.shift();

  //The `while` loop ends here
  }

  //Now that we have all the candidates, let's find the shortest path!
  if (openList.length !== 0) {

    //Start with the destination node
    let testNode = destinationNode;
    shortestPath.push(testNode);

    //Work backwards through the node parents
    //until the start node is found
    while (testNode !== startNode) {

      //Step through the parents of each node,
      //starting with the destination node and ending with the start node
      testNode = testNode.parent;

      //Add the node to the beginning of the array
      shortestPath.unshift(testNode);

      //...and then loop again to the next node's parent till you
      //reach the end of the path
    }
  }

  //Return an array of nodes that link together to form
  //the shortest path
  return shortestPath;
}
```

Using the shortestPath Function

In the chapter's source files, you'll find a folder called shortestPath.html. Run the program, and you'll see an alien character sitting in a simple maze environment. Click anywhere with the mouse, and the program will draw the shortest path from the alien's position to the mouse's location, as shown in Figure 6-18.

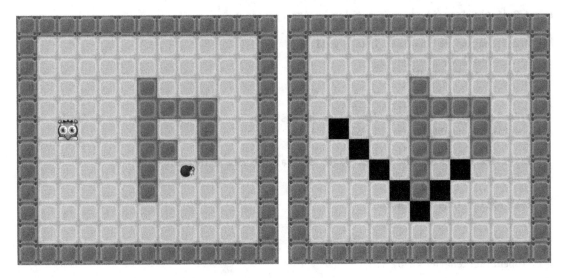

Figure 6-18. *Click anywhere to draw the shortest path*

This program works by calculating the shortest path between the alien sprite and the mouse's location. As you've learned, the shortestPath function returns an array of nodes. Each node has a row and column property, and we can use that information to display a black square sprite on the screen for every node in the array.

Here's the relevant code from the program's setup function that does this. An array called currentPathSprites is populated with black square sprites, which match the shortest path nodes, each time the mouse pointer is released.

```
//An array to store the sprites that will be used to display
//the shortest path
currentPathSprites = [];

//The mouse pointer's `release` function runs the code that
//calculates the shortest path and draws that sprites that
//represent it
g.pointer.release = () => {

  //calculate the shortest path
  let path = shortestPath(
    getIndex(alien.x, alien.y, 64, 64, 13),          //Start map index
    getIndex(g.pointer.x, g.pointer.y, 64, 64, 13),  //End index
    wallMapArray,                                    //Map array
    13,                                              //Map width
    [2, 3],                                          //Obstacle gids
    "manhattan"                                      //Heuristic
  );
```

```
//Use Hexi's `remove` method to remove any possible
//sprites in the `currentPathSprites` array
g.remove(currentPathSprites);

//Display the shortest path
path.forEach(node => {

  //Figure out the x and y location of each square in the path by
  //multiplying the node's `column` and `row` by the height, in
  //pixels, of each square: 64
  let x = node.column * 64,
      y = node.row * 64;

  //Create the square sprite and set it to the x and y location
  //we calculated above
  let square = g.rectangle(64, 64, "black");
  square.x = x;
  square.y = y;

  //Push the sprites into the `currentPath` array,
  //so that we can easily remove them the next time
  //the mouse is clicked
  currentPathSprites.push(square);
});
};
```

Just for completeness, you'll notice that the code above uses a convenience function called remove that's built into the rendering engine. Its job is to remove single sprites or any sprites an array of sprites, from the renderer. Here's the remove function that does this work, just in case you need to do anything similar in your own programs:

```
function remove(...sprites) {

  //Remove sprites that's aren't in an array
  if (!(sprites[0] instanceof Array)) {
    if (sprites.length > 1) {
      sprites.forEach(sprite => {
        sprite.parent.removeChild(sprite);
      });
    } else {
      sprites[0].parent.removeChild(sprites[0]);
    }
  }

  //Remove sprites in an array of sprites
  else {
    let spritesArray = sprites[0];
    if (spritesArray.length > 0) {
      for (let i = spritesArray.length - 1; i >= 0; i--) {
        let sprite = spritesArray[i];
        sprite.parent.removeChild(sprite);
```

```
        spritesArray.splice(spritesArray.indexOf(sprite), 1);
      }
    }
  }
}
```

You can see that as long as you have the `shortestPath` array, there are many ways that you can use it. In the examples ahead, I'll show you how you can use it to make a game character walk through the maze. But first, let's look at a topic that I've been strategically avoiding until now: heuristics.

Understanding Heuristics

There will usually be more than one shortest path to a destination, as shown in Figure 6-19.

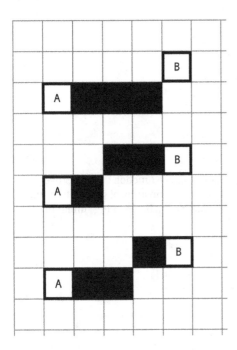

Figure 6-19. *All three paths are the same length, but the route they choose is different*

None of the paths is any better or worse than the other, and they all have the same cost. But each has a unique style. This style depends on the heuristic that A* uses to calculate the path.

A **heuristic** is a mini-algorithm whose job is to work out distances based on a simple formula. Three famous heuristics are often used with A*: Manhattan, Euclidean, and Diagonal. Figure 6-20 illustrates the different paths that each heuristic in the `shortestPath` function produces. Which do you prefer?

Manhattan

Diagonal

Euclidean

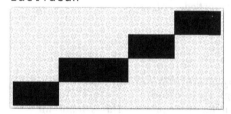

Figure 6-20. *Different heuristics produce different paths*

The shortestPath function selects which heuristic to use based on the last argument supplied to it.

```
let path = shortestPath(
  getIndex(alien.x, alien.y, 64, 64, 13),
  getIndex(g.pointer.x, g.pointer.y, 64, 64, 13),
  wallMapArray,
  13,
  [2, 3],
  "manhattan"
);
```

A switch statement in the while loop finds the value of H by delegating the work to whichever heuristic method was specified.

```
let h;
switch (heuristic) {
  case "manhattan":
    h = manhattan(testNode, destinationNode);
    break;
```

```
  case "euclidean":
    h = euclidean(testNode, destinationNode);
    break;

  case "diagonal":
    h = diagonal(testNode, destinationNode);
    break;

  default:
    throw new Error("Oops! It looks like you misspelled the name of the heuristic");
}
```

Each heuristic method calculates the distance between the start and end point in different ways. The Manhattan method is simplest. It just adds together the rows and columns, and multiplies the sum by the cost. It ignores any possible diagonal shortcuts.

```
let manhattan = (testNode, destinationNode) => {
  let h
    = Math.abs(testNode.row - destinationNode.row)
    * straightCost + Math.abs(testNode.column - destinationNode.column)
    * straightCost;
  return h;
};
```

It's called Manhattan because if you were walking down the streets of New York City (Manhatten island), you wouldn't be able to take a shortcut diagonally through any city block.

Ignoring possible diagonal routes makes the Manhattan heuristic fast to process. This is important because A* is an extremely CPU-hungry algorithm. If you need to do pathfinding for a lot of game characters on each frame, Manhattan will save you some performance impact. However, because it doesn't account for diagonal routes, it may not always guarantee the absolute shortest path.

The Euclidean method uses the Pythagorean theorem to calculate the distance.

```
let euclidean = (testNode, destinationNode) => {
  let vx = destinationNode.column - testNode.column,
    vy = destinationNode.row - testNode.row,
    h = Math.floor(Math.sqrt(vx * vx + vy * vy) * straightCost);
  return h;
};
```

The Euclidean method does account for diagonals, so it produces a very natural-looking path. However, it's a little slower to process than the Manhattan method because of that hungry Math.sqrt method.

The Diagonal method compensates for the costs of moving straight across or diagonally, so it ends up with a very accurate cost estimate. This means that A* may need to do less searching and produce a faster result, and it will definitely produce the shortest possible path.

```
let diagonal = (testNode, destinationNode) => {
  let vx = Math.abs(destinationNode.column - testNode.column),
    vy = Math.abs(destinationNode.row - testNode.row),
    h = 0;
```

```
  if (vx > vy) {
    h = Math.floor(diagonalCost * vy + straightCost * (vx - vy));
  } else {
    h = Math.floor(diagonalCost * vx + straightCost * (vy - vx));
  }
  return h;
};
```

There's no one right heuristic to use. You just need to decide which produces the kind of path that seems the most natural for the game you're making.

Rounding Corners

There's a potential problem with our current A* algorithm: it calculates the shortest path by taking a diagonal shortcut between cells. This is accurate, but it poses a problem for maze games. In most maze games, you'll want your characters to walk around the edges of walls, so cutting corners diagonally would look strange. Figure 6-21 illustrates this dilemma.

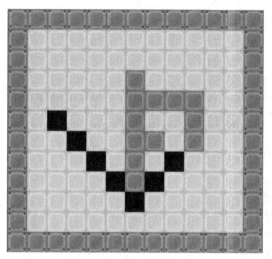 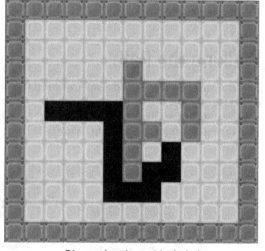

Diagonal nodes included   Diagonal nodes not included

Figure 6-21. Maze game paths should usually not cut diagonally around corners

There's a simple solution to preventing paths from taking diagonal shortcuts around corners: just don't check for any nodes that are diagonally adjacent to the current center test node. In the current surroundingNodes function from the code in our example A* implementation, all eight nodes surrounding the current center node are tested:

```
let allSurroundingNodes = [
  nodeMap[index - mapWidthInTiles - 1],
  nodeMap[index - mapWidthInTiles],
  nodeMap[index - mapWidthInTiles + 1],
  nodeMap[index - 1],
```

```
  nodeMap[index + 1],
  nodeMap[index + mapWidthInTiles - 1],
  nodeMap[index + mapWidthInTiles],
  nodeMap[index + mapWidthInTiles + 1]
];
```

```
let validSurroundingNodes = allSurroundingNodes.filter(node => {/*...*/});
```

To prevent diagonals, just test the nodes directly above, below, and to the right and left of the center node:

```
let crossSurroundingNodes = [
  nodeMap[index - mapWidthInTiles],
  nodeMap[index - 1],
  nodeMap[index + 1],
  nodeMap[index + mapWidthInTiles],
];
```

```
let validSurroundingNodes = crossSurroundingNodes.filter(node => {/*...*/});
```

And that's all there is to it!

Walking the Path

Now that we know how to find a path, we need to teach our game characters how to walk along it. You'll find a working example of this in the walkPath.html program. Click anywhere in the maze, and the alien sprite will take the shortest route to get there. The A* algorithm uses the modification we just looked at to allow the path to round corners, as shown in Figure 6-22.

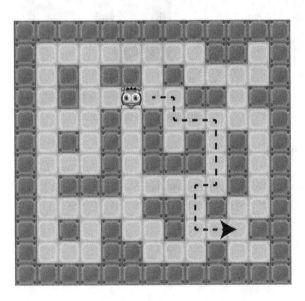

Figure 6-22. *Click anywhere on the map, and the game character will walk there*

This works by using the shortestPath function to create a new 2D array of x/y points. These points are called **way points**. Each way point represents the x/y location of each node in the path. Those points are then used to tell the sprite which direction to move in. Let's look at the code that makes all of this work.

First, the setup function defines the pointer's release method. It captures the pointer's x and y position in two new variables called destinationX and destinationY. It also sets a Boolean variable called calculateNewPath variable to true to flag that a new path should be calculated at the next opportunity. The setup function also defines a variable called wayPoints2DArray that will be used later to store the pairs of x/y way points.

```
//An array that will be used to store sub-arrays of
//x/y position value pairs that we're going to use
//to change the velocity of the alien sprite
wayPoints2DArray = [];

//A Boolean that will be set to true when the pointer
//is clicked, and set to false when the new path
//is calculated
calculateNewPath = false;

//The pointer's `release` method, which is called when the left mouse button
//or touch point is released
g.pointer.release = () => {

  //Set the new path's destination to the pointer's
  //current x and y position
  destinationX = g.pointer.x;
  destinationY = g.pointer.y;

  //Set `calculateNewPath` to true
  calculateNewPath = true;
};
```

The rest of the important code is in the game loop, which, in the implementation we've been using in this book, happens inside a function called play. Here's the complete code, with comments explaining how each section works. (This code uses the isCenteredOverCell and getIndex helper functions that you learned in earlier chapters.)

```
function play() {

  //Find out if the alien is centered over a tile cell
  if (isCenteredOverCell(alien)) {

    //If `calculateNewPath` has been set to `true` by the pointer,
    //find the new shortest path between the alien and the pointer's
    //x and y position (`destinationX` and `destinationY`)
    if (calculateNewPath) {

      //calculate the shortest path
      let path = shortestPath(
        getIndex(alien.centerX, alien.centerY, 64, 64, 13), //Start index
        getIndex(destinationX, destinationY, 64, 64, 13),   //End index
        wallMapArray,                                        //Map array
        13,                                                  //Map width
```

```
    [2, 3],                                        //Gid array
    "manhattan"                                    //Heuristic
);

//Remove the first node of the `path` array. That's because we
//don't need it: the alien sprite's current location and the
//first node in the `path` array share the same location.
//In the code ahead we're going to tell the alien sprite to move
//from its current location, to first new node in the path.
path.shift();

//If the path isn't empty, fill the `wayPoints2DArray` with
//sub arrays of x/y position value pairs.
if (path.length !== 0) {

    //Get a 2D array of x/y points
    wayPoints2DArray = path.map(node => {

        //Figure out the x and y location of each square in the path by
        //multiplying the node's `column` and `row` by the height, in
        //pixels, of each cell: 64
        let x = node.column * 64,
            y = node.row * 64;

        //Return a sub-array containing the x and y position of each node
        return [x, y];
    });
}

    //Set `calculateNewPath` to `false` so that this block of code.
    //won't run again inside the game loop. (It can be set to `true`
    //again by clicking the pointer.)
    calculateNewPath = false;
}

//Set the alien's new velocity based on
//the alien's relative x/y position to the current, next, way point.
//Because we are always going to
//remove a way point element after we set this new
//velocity, the first element in the `wayPoints2DArray`
//will always refer to the next way point that the
//alien sprite has to move to
if (wayPoints2DArray.length !== 0) {

    //Left
    if (wayPoints2DArray[0][0] < alien.x) {
        alien.vx = -4;
        alien.vy = 0;

    //Right
    } else if (wayPoints2DArray[0][0] > alien.x) {
```

```
      alien.vx = 4;
      alien.vy = 0;

    //Up
    } else if (wayPoints2DArray[0][1] < alien.y) {
      alien.vx = 0;
      alien.vy = -4;

    //Down
    } else if (wayPoints2DArray[0][1] > alien.y) {
      alien.vx = 0;
      alien.vy = 4;
    }

    //Remove the current way point, so that next time around
    //the first element in the `wayPoints2DArray` will correctly refer
    //to the next way point that that alien sprite has
    //to move to
    wayPoints2DArray.shift();

  //If there are no way points remaining,
  //set the alien's velocity to 0
  } else {
    alien.vx = 0;
    alien.vy = 0;
  }
}

//Move the alien sprite based on the new velocity
alien.x += alien.vx;
alien.y += alien.vy;
}
```

In this example, a new path is calculated whenever the user clicks the mouse, but you can change this in your own games this so that the path is calculated whenever anything significant happens that should cause a sprite to change direction.

Extending and Customizing A*

You will definitely need to invest a bit of time into getting comfortable using A* and understanding all its subtleties. But it's certainly worth the effort, as it's a cornerstone game design technique that is used on all platforms in most game genres.

A big part of A*'s appeal is its flexibility. As you've seen, you can produce a different kind of path just by switching the heuristic. But it's not just the heuristics that make A* as flexible as it is. Let's look at a few of the other possibilities the A* algorithm offers.

Variable Terrain

In this chapter's examples, we've had only one type of obstacle: walls. However, you may have different kinds of obstacles in your games, not all of which are impenetrable.

What if you had a game with a mud pit? Characters could still move through the mud, but it would slow them down. You could modify A* so that nodes containing mud have a high costs. For example, give your G costs an extra 20 or 30 points when A* encounters a mud node. A* would then calculate whether it's faster to go around the mud or take the shortcut through it.

Strategy games use this technique all the time. Troops need to consider whether it's better to stick to the plains and travel fast, or take their time crossing mountains. This analysis is all done by A*'s cost analysis of different kinds of moves.

Influence Map

Here's another interesting problem that's solvable with A*. Imagine that you have enemy AI characters that are using A* to find the best exit to a dungeon. The only problem is that you've discovered that you can easily rack up a high score by hiding near that exit and knocking off each enemy as it blindly stumbles by. The enemies have no way of warning their friends that, although this might be the shortest route, it's also extremely dangerous.

You can fix this by using what's called an **influence map**. If an area of the game world becomes particularly dangerous, make those nodes a very high cost. When A* searches for a path, it will avoid those expensive, dangerous areas.

You can also extend this concept to solve the problem of many enemies following the same path. In many games, it will seem very unnatural if all the enemies choose the same shortest path. You can force enemies to take a different path by tracking the path that each chooses, and assigning high costs to those nodes. A* will then avoid nodes and paths that have already been chosen by other enemies.

Dijkstra's Algorithm

Earlier, I mentioned that A* was a modification of Dijkstra's algorithm. There is one good reason to use Dijkstra's algorithm over A*: when you don't know the final destination of the path.

The only difference between A* and Dijkstra's algorithm is that A* adds heuristics. In Dijkstra's algorithm, H always has a value of zero. The means that when Dijkstra's algorithm starts looking for a path, it doesn't know in which direction to start looking. It must do a lot more searching than A* to find the goal.

But what if you have a game where you're not sure where the character's final destination will be? Imagine that you're designing a strategy or resource management game and your villagers need to collect strawberries. There are four strawberry bushes around the town, but you don't know which bush is the closest. If you use Dijkstra's algorithm, it will search outward in all directions until it finds the first one. If you use A*, you will need to calculate four different paths to each bush and choose the shortest. Dijkstra's algorithm saves you from having to do this, so it would be a better choice in this case.

If you want to use Dijkstra's algorithm rather than A*, just assign 0 to all the H costs. The rest of the A* code will be the same.

Don't reinvent the wheel! This chapter was written so that you completely understand how A* works. It's been intended to help you customize it, rewrite it, and modify it however you want. But, there are plenty of high-quality, open source implementations of A* in JavaScript that might be more performant, more flexible, or easier to implement for your use case. Easystar.js and Pathfinding.js are good places to start.

Summary

This chapter has presented a brief introduction to pathfinding, which should get you thinking about what's possible for your own games. Adventure games, strategy games, and any games that require sophisticated AI will benefit from these techniques. You've learned everything you need to know to implement your own A* pathfinding algorithm from scratch and how to use it to move sprites around your tile-based game world.

But we're not done with tile-based games by any means! In the next chapter you're going to learn a few more secrets of tile-based game design: how to use tiles to easily create surprisingly sophisticated, autonomous AI entitles, and how to implement an efficient broadphase collision detection system.

CHAPTER 7

■ ■ ■

More Fun with Tile-Based Games

Much of this book has been an exploration of how a tile-based approach to game design can help you solve some complex problems in an easy and efficient way. It can help you improve and simplify everything from level design, collision, game logic, and AI to pathfinding. But this book would not be complete without an exploration of two more tile-based design strategies that you'll be sure to find a lot of use for in your games:

- **Hidden game data**: You can hide special information about your game inside map cells that can be used to create sophisticated Artificial Intelligence entities. In this chapter, you'll see how by creating an autonomous self-driving car for a simple race-car game prototype.

- **Broadphase collision detection**: Improve the performance of computation-heavy physics based games by only checking for collisions between objects that are likely to collide. You'll learn how by implementing a versatile and lightweight collision system called a **spatial grid**.

So buckle up and start your engine – we're ready to hit the road!

Using Extra Game Data for AI Systems

We're going to start this chapter with a look at how to create a computer-controlled car for a race-car driving game. But before we do that, let's find out how can you create a human-controlled race car that can navigate around a track using the keyboard. Run the drivingGame.html file in this chapter's source files for a working prototype, show in Figure 7-1. Use the keyboard to drive the car around the track.

© Rex van der Spuy 2017
R. van der Spuy, *The Advanced Game Developer's Toolkit*, DOI 10.1007/978-1-4842-1097-0_7

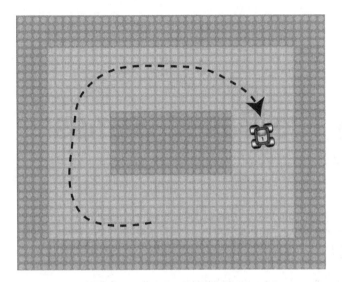

Figure 7-1. *Use the keyboard to drive the car around the track, but be careful not to get stuck in the grass*

This little prototype also implements one of the most annoying, must-have features of driving games: if you drive off the track, your car will get stuck in the grass and slow down. Thanks to the elegance of our tile-based design system, this was a very easy feature to implement, which you'll find out all about in the sections ahead. But first, let's take a quick look at how this little prototype was put together.

Below you'll find the entire JavaScript file that makes this game work. Most of the code will be very familiar, so consider it a quick review of the basics of the tile-based game world building. What's new is the player car's control system. The code listens for keyboard arrow key presses: if the up arrow is pressed, a moveForward Boolean is set to true; if the right and left arrow keys are pressed the car's rotationSpeed is set. These values are then used in the game loop (the play function) to rotate and move the car. Here's the complete code listing with comments that explain exactly how everything works.

```
//Load any assets used in this game
let thingsToLoad = [
  "images/tileSet.png",
];

//Create a new Hexi instance, and start it
let g = hexi(640, 512, setup, thingsToLoad);

//Scale the canvas to the maximum browser dimensions
g.scaleToWindow();

//Start the game engine
g.start();

//Intiialize variables
let car, world;
```

```
function setup() {

  //Create the `world` container that defines our tile-based world
  world = g.group();

  //Set the `tileWidth` and `tileHeight` of each tile, in pixels
  world.tileWidth = 64;
  world.tileHeight = 64;

  //Define the width and height of the world, in tiles
  world.widthInTiles = 10;
  world.heightInTiles = 8;

  //Create the world layers
  world.layers = [

    //The environment layer. `1` represents the grass,
    //`2` represents the track
    [
      1, 1, 1, 1, 1, 1, 1, 1, 1, 1,
      1, 2, 2, 2, 2, 2, 2, 2, 2, 1,
      1, 2, 2, 2, 2, 2, 2, 2, 2, 1,
      1, 2, 2, 1, 1, 1, 1, 2, 2, 1,
      1, 2, 2, 1, 1, 1, 1, 2, 2, 1,
      1, 2, 2, 2, 2, 2, 2, 2, 2, 1,
      1, 2, 2, 2, 2, 2, 2, 2, 2, 1,
      1, 1, 1, 1, 1, 1, 1, 1, 1, 1
    ],

    //The character layer. `3` represents the car
    //`0` represents an empty cell which won't contain any
    //sprites
    [
      0, 0, 0, 0, 0, 0, 0, 0, 0, 0,
      0, 0, 3, 0, 0, 0, 0, 0, 0, 0,
      0, 0, 0, 0, 0, 0, 0, 0, 0, 0,
      0, 0, 0, 0, 0, 0, 0, 0, 0, 0,
      0, 0, 0, 0, 0, 0, 0, 0, 0, 0,
      0, 0, 0, 0, 0, 0, 0, 0, 0, 0,
      0, 0, 0, 0, 0, 0, 0, 0, 0, 0,
      0, 0, 0, 0, 0, 0, 0, 0, 0, 0
    ]
  ];

  //Build the game world by looping through each
  //of the layer arrays one after the other
  world.layers.forEach(layer => {

    //Loop through each array element
    layer.forEach((gid, index) => {
```

165

```
    //If the cell isn't empty (0) then create a sprite
    if (gid !== 0) {

      //Find the column and row that the sprite is on and also
      //its x and y pixel values that match column and row position
      let column, row, x, y;
      column = index % world.widthInTiles;
      row = Math.floor(index / world.widthInTiles);
      x = column * world.tileWidth;
      y = row * world.tileHeight;

      //Next, create a different sprite based on what its
      //`gid` number is
      let sprite;
      switch (gid) {

        //The track
        case 1:
          sprite = g.sprite(g.frame("images/tileSet.png", 192, 64, 64, 64));
          break;

        //The grass
        case 2:
          sprite = g.sprite(g.frame("images/tileSet.png", 192, 0, 64, 64));
          break;

        //The car
        case 3:
          sprite = g.sprite(g.frame("images/tileSet.png", 192, 192, 48, 48));
          car = sprite;
      }

      //Position the sprite using the calculated `x` and `y` values
      //that match its column and row in the tile map
      sprite.x = x;
      sprite.y = y;

      //Add the sprite to the `world` container
      world.addChild(sprite);
    }
  });
});

//Add some physics properties to the car
car.vx = 0;
car.vy = 0;
car.accelerationX = 0.2;
car.accelerationY = 0.2;
car.rotationSpeed = 0;
car.friction = 0.96;
car.speed = 0;
```

```
//Set the car's center rotation point to the middle of the sprite
car.setPivot(0.5, 0.5);

//Whether or not the car should move forward
car.moveForward = false;

//Define the arrow keys to move the car
let leftArrow = g.keyboard(37),
  upArrow = g.keyboard(38),
  rightArrow = g.keyboard(39),
  downArrow = g.keyboard(40);

//Set the car's `rotationSpeed` to -0.1 (to rotate left) if the
//left arrow key is being pressed
leftArrow.press = () => {
  car.rotationSpeed = -0.05;
};

//If the left arrow key is released and the right arrow
//key isn't being pressed down, set the `rotationSpeed` to 0
leftArrow.release = () => {
  if (!rightArrow.isDown) car.rotationSpeed = 0;
};

//Do the same for the right arrow key, but set
//the `rotationSpeed` to 0.1 (to rotate right)
rightArrow.press = () => {
  car.rotationSpeed = 0.05;
};

rightArrow.release = () => {
  if (!leftArrow.isDown) car.rotationSpeed = 0;
};

//Set `car.moveForward` to `true` if the up arrow key is
//pressed, and set it to `false` if it's released
upArrow.press = () => {
  car.moveForward = true;
};
upArrow.release = () => {
  car.moveForward = false;
};

//Start the game loop by setting the game state to `play`
g.state = play;
}

//The game loop
function play() {

  //Use the `rotationSpeed` to set the car's rotation
  car.rotation += car.rotationSpeed;
```

```
//If `car.moveForward` is `true`, increase the speed
if (car.moveForward) {
  car.speed += 0.05;
}

//If `car.moveForward` is `false`, use
//friction to slow the car down
else {
  car.speed *= car.friction;
}

//Use the `speed` value to figure out the acceleration in the
//direction of the car's rotation
car.accelerationX = car.speed * Math.cos(car.rotation);
car.accelerationY = car.speed * Math.sin(car.rotation);

//Apply the acceleration and friction to the car's velocity
car.vx = car.accelerationX
car.vy = car.accelerationY
car.vx *= car.friction;
car.vy *= car.friction

//Apply the car's velocity to its position to make the car move
car.x += car.vx;
car.y += car.vy;

//Slow the car down if it's stuck in the grass

//First find the car's map index position (using
//the `getIndex` helper function)
let carIndex = getIndex(car.x, car.y, 64, 64, 10);

//Get a reference to the race track map
let trackMap = world.layers[0];

//Slow the car if it's on a grass tile (gid 1) by setting
//the car's friction to 0.25, to make it sluggish
if (trackMap[carIndex] === 1) {
  car.friction = 0.25;
}

//If the car isn't on a grass tile, restore its
//original friction value
else {
  car.friction = 0.96;
}

}
```

The last few lines above are what slow the car down when it drives into the grass. The code compares the car's index position on the map. If it's on a grass tile (a gid of 1), then the car's friction is increased by setting the multiplier to 0.25. Otherwise, the car must be on the track, so the friction multiplier is set to normal, 0.96.

Storing Hidden Game Data in Arrays

The next step is to add an AI controlled car that can navigate the track on its own. To do this, we're going to create a new map array that stores information about which direction the AI car should turn, depending on where on the track it is. This data is "hidden" because the player of the game isn't aware it's there – it's just used by the game's AI system to make decisions.

You've seen how map arrays are not just used for plotting tiles, but also to help interpret the game world. In the driving game example we just looked at, the grass data in the array not only helped plot the grass tile on the screen, but also played a crucial role in the game logic. The power of tile-based games is that map array data holds meaningful information, which can be used in the game for everything from the display to the AI system.

You can take this one step further. What if you stored data in the arrays that contained more information about the game world other than just what you can see on the screen?

Imagine that you're creating a fantasy role-playing game where players can cast spells that affect part of the game world. The Bard character casts a spell of Discordant Cacophony that makes all the enemies run away from the area of the game map where the spell is cast. How will you describe this information to the game?

You could create a "spell map" that matches the size of the game world. You could mark all the parts of the world that are affected by Discordant Cacophony with some kind of code, like 1.

```
let spellMap = [
  0,0,0,0,0,0,0,0,0,0,0,
  0,0,0,0,0,0,0,0,0,0,0,
  0,0,0,0,1,0,0,0,0,0,0,
  0,0,0,1,1,1,0,0,0,0,0,
  0,0,0,1,1,1,0,0,0,0,0,
  0,0,0,0,1,0,0,0,0,0,0,
  0,0,0,0,0,0,0,0,0,0,0,
  0,0,0,0,0,0,0,0,0,0,0
];
```

Enemies could then take this information into account and decide whether or not they want to risk ruptured eardrums by entering any of those tiles.

This information isn't visual; it's just used by the logic of the game. When you start becoming comfortable thinking in a tile-based way about your games, you'll find that many otherwise complex problems can be solved easily with arrays of game data like this.

So how can we add some hidden game data like this to help us create an AI controlled race car?

Adding an AI Controlled Car

Run the aiDrivingGame.html program, shown in Figure 7-2. Now you have an opponent to play against: an AI-controlled robot car that does its best to race you around the track.

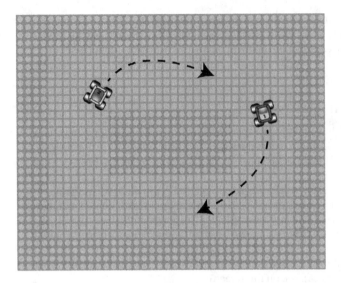

Figure 7-2. *Race an AI opponent car around the track*

The AI car isn't following a pre-scripted animation, and it doesn't have a dedicated AI controller. Instead, it's reading an array of numbers that tells it how it should try to angle itself depending on which map cell it's in. It's following an invisible "angle map." The angle map is the game's third map layer, and it defines angles, in degrees, for each cell in the map.

```
[
  45,   45,  45,  45,  45,  45,  45,  45, 135, 135,
 315,    0,   0,   0,   0,   0,   0,  90, 135, 135,
 315,    0,   0,   0,   0,   0,   0,  90, 135, 135,
 315,  315, 270, 315, 315, 315, 315,  90,  90, 135,
 315,  315, 270, 135, 135, 135, 135,  90,  90, 135,
 315,  315, 270, 180, 180, 180, 180, 180, 225, 135,
 315,  315, 270, 180, 180, 180, 180, 180, 225, 135,
 315,  270, 270, 225, 225, 225, 225, 225, 225, 225
]
```

These angles tell the AI car at what angle it should attempt to orient itself depending on which cell it's in. (0 degrees points directly to the right, at the 3 o'clock position.) You can think of these angle values as little arrows that are pointing in the direction the AI car needs to travel in, as illustrated in Figure 7-3.

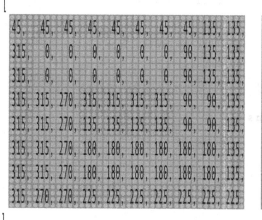 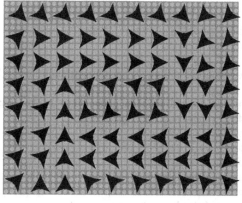

Figure 7-3. *An array of angles determines the direction that the AI car should try and orient itself*

All the AI car needs to do to drive around the track is rotate itself to the optimum angle of the cell that it's currently in. And, just for fun, the code adds a bit of random variation to those angles, within plus or minus 20 degrees. That randomness makes the AI car's driving appear much more natural, like an imperfect human driver. Let's walk through the new code that makes this happen.

The code first declares three new global variables: aiCar, previousMapAngle, and targetAngle.

```
let car, world, aiCar, previousMapAngle, targetAngle;
```

Then the setup function creates the new data that game will need. The AI car is added to the world object's second map layer, represented by the number 4.

```
[
  0, 0, 0, 0, 0, 0, 0, 0, 0, 0,
  0, 0, 3, 0, 0, 0, 0, 0, 0, 0,
  0, 0, 4, 0, 0, 0, 0, 0, 0, 0,
  0, 0, 0, 0, 0, 0, 0, 0, 0, 0,
  0, 0, 0, 0, 0, 0, 0, 0, 0, 0,
  0, 0, 0, 0, 0, 0, 0, 0, 0, 0,
  0, 0, 0, 0, 0, 0, 0, 0, 0, 0,
  0, 0, 0, 0, 0, 0, 0, 0, 0, 0
],
```

The angle array is then added as the world object's third map layer.

```
[
   45,  45,  45,  45,  45,  45,  45,  45, 135, 135,
  315,   0,   0,   0,   0,   0,   0,  90, 135, 135,
  315,   0,   0,   0,   0,   0,   0,  90, 135, 135,
  315, 315, 270, 315, 315, 315, 315,  90,  90, 135,
  315, 315, 270, 135, 135, 135, 135,  90,  90, 135,
  315, 315, 270, 180, 180, 180, 180, 180, 180, 135,
  315, 315, 270, 180, 180, 180, 180, 180, 180, 135,
  315, 270, 270, 225, 225, 225, 225, 225, 225, 225
]
```

The switch statement that builds the world creates the new aiCar sprite like this.

```
case 4:
  sprite = g.sprite(g.frame("images/tileSet.png", 192, 128, 48, 48));
  aiCar = sprite;
```

The properties of both car sprites are then initialized.

```
//A function to add physics properties to the cars
let addCarProperties = carSprite => {
  carSprite.vx = 0;
  carSprite.vy = 0;
  carSprite.accelerationX = 0.2;
  carSprite.accelerationY = 0.2;
  carSprite.rotationSpeed = 0;
  carSprite.friction = 0.96;
  carSprite.speed = 0;

  //Center the rotation point
  carSprite.setPivot(0.5, 0.5);

  //Whether or not the car should move forward
  carSprite.moveForward = false;
};

//Add physics properties to the player's car
addCarProperties(car);

//Add physics properties and set it to move forward
//when the game begins
addCarProperties(aiCar);
aiCar.moveForward = true;
```

The rest of the new code is in the play function. It figures out what the AI car's new target angle should be, attempts to rotate the car toward that angle, adds some random variation, and moves the car using its physics properties. All the details of how this code works is in the comments.

```
//If `aICar.moveForward` is `true`, increase the speed as long
//it is under the maximum speed limit of 3
if (aiCar.moveForward && aiCar.speed <= 3) {
  aiCar.speed += 0.08;
}

//Find the AI car's current angle, in degrees
let currentAngle = aiCar.rotation * (180 / Math.PI);

//Constrain the calculated angle to a value between 0 and 360
currentAngle = currentAngle + Math.ceil(-currentAngle / 360) * 360;

//Find out its index position on the map
let aiCarIndex = getIndex(aiCar.x, aiCar.y, 64, 64, 10);
```

```
//Find out what the target angle is for that map position
let angleMap = world.layers[2];
let mapAngle = angleMap[aiCarIndex];

//Add an optional random variation of 20 degrees each time the aiCar
//encounters a new map angle
if (mapAngle !== previousMapAngle) {
  targetAngle = mapAngle + randomInt(-20, 20);
  previousMapAngle = mapAngle;
}

//If you don't want any random variation in the iaCar's angle
//replace the above if statement with this line of code:
//targetAngle = mapAngle;

//Calculate the difference between the current
//angle and the target angle
let difference = currentAngle - targetAngle;

//Figure out whether to turn the car left or right
if (difference > 0 && difference < 180) {

  //Turn left
  aiCar.rotationSpeed = -0.03;
} else {

  //Turn right
  aiCar.rotationSpeed = 0.03;
}

//Use the `rotationSpeed` to set the car's rotation
aiCar.rotation += aiCar.rotationSpeed;

//Use the `speed` value to figure out the acceleration in the
//direction of the aiCar's rotation
aiCar.accelerationX = aiCar.speed * Math.cos(aiCar.rotation);
aiCar.accelerationY = aiCar.speed * Math.sin(aiCar.rotation);

//Apply the acceleration and friction to the aiCar's velocity
aiCar.vx = aiCar.accelerationX
aiCar.vy = aiCar.accelerationY
aiCar.vx *= aiCar.friction;
aiCar.vy *= aiCar.friction;

//Apply the aiCar's velocity to its position to make the aiCar move
aiCar.x += aiCar.vx;
aiCar.y += aiCar.vy;
```

But there's one more thing! To make this a fair game, we also need to slow down the AI car if it runs into the grass. This bit of code near the end of play function that does that job.

```
//Get a reference to the race track map
let trackMap = world.layers[0];

//Slow the aiCar if it's on a grass tile (gid 1) by setting
//its friction to 0.25, to make it sluggish
if (trackMap[aiCarIndex] === 1) {
  aiCar.friction = 0.25;

  //If the car isn't on a grass tile, restore its
  //original friction value
} else {
  aiCar.friction = 0.96;
}
```

Run the example file, and it you'll see that it can be quite amusing to watch the AI car drive into the grass and struggle to free itself.

This basic prototype encapsulates all the basic techniques you need to know to build a full-featured racecar game with AI opponents. Here are some ideas you could use to take these ideas further:

- Make a variety of AI cars at different skill levels just by varying or randomizing the rotationSpeed number.

- Have different AI cars using different angle maps to vary the difficulty and keep things unpredictable for the human player.

- Analyze how well human players did after each race, and make the game more or less difficult to keep it challenging.

- Give the AI cars a collision avoidance system so that they steer away from other cars if they get too close to them. You can find out everything you need to build such a system in this book's companion, *Advanced Game Design with HTML5 and JavaScript* (Apress, 2015).

You'll surely find countless more solutions to tricky problems once you start thinking about storing and using game data in the way you've learned how to do in this chapter so far.

Broadphase and Narrowphase Collision

There are two different general approaches to handling collision detection in games, known as **broadphase** and **narrowphase** collision.

- **Broadphase collision**: Checking whether sprites are in the general area of the collision, such as the tile-based collision we examined in detail in earlier chapters. Its advantage is that it's an extremely performance efficient way to check for collisions between large numbers of sprites. That's because it just does simple array look-ups, and doesn't have to do any heavy math processing.

- **Narrowphase collision**: Checking the precise geometry of the sprites to find out if their shapes overlap. Its advantage is that, because it's extremely precise, narrowphase collision is essential for physics simulations, such as checking for collisions between two billiard balls. Its disadvantage is that because it taxes the CPU with a lot of math, it's very performance hungry. It can be slow if you're checking collisions between large numbers of sprites. Although how to implement a narrowphase collision system is not covered in this book, you can find everything you need to know to build such a system from scratch in *Advanced Game Design with HTML5 and JavaScript*.

These two collision systems represent the foundations of collision detection in all video games. How do you decide which to use? Often the choice is easy: if you need physics, use narrowphase; otherwise use broadphase. But there's a gray area!

What if you're making a game in which thousands of circles need to bounce against each other? You try implementing a physics-heavy narrowphase collision system, but your frame rate drops to 5 frames per second. Way too slow! So you implement a broadphase collision system and easily get 60 frames per second. But now your circles visibly overlap each other before they bounce apart, which looks extremely imprecise. What should you do?

Use both broadphase *and* narrowphase collision together! Break down your collision system into two steps:

1. **Broadphase check**: First use broadphase collision to find out whether the sprites you're interested in are in the general vicinity of each other and might actually be close enough to touch during this animation frame.

2. **Narrowphase check**: If your broadphase check determines that, yes, a collision is possible, run a much more precise, but more CPU expense narrowphase check.

There are many ways that you can implement this two-stage collision strategy, but I'm going to show you the simplest, most useful, and usually most performance efficient one: the **spatial grid**.

The Spatial Grid

To create a spatial grid, divide your game world up into cells. How big should those cells be? It should be as large as one of your sprites is likely to move during one animation frame. For example, let's say you're creating a marble game, and you determine that none of your marble sprites will ever move faster than 64 frames per second. That means you can use a spatial grid in which each cell is 64 pixels wide and 64 pixels high. Figure 7-4 shows what this grid would look like if your game screen is 512 by 512 pixels.

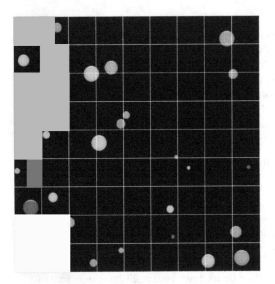

Figure 7-4. Divide your world up into cells

In a standard narrowphase collision system, every sprite would be checked for a collision against every other sprite in the entire game. That's wasteful, because collisions will be checked between sprites that are on completely opposite sides of the screen, even if they have no chance of ever colliding. But, if you're using a spatial grid, your collision checks are much more focused. For each sprite, you just need to check for collisions between it and the sprites that are in the cells directly adjacent to it.

For example, take a look at Figure 7-5. In the middle left of the screen is a large white circle. The cell that white circle is in, combined with the eight cells that surround it, represents the circle's **collision zone**. This collision zone is the only area on the screen where this sprite has any chance of colliding with any other sprites.

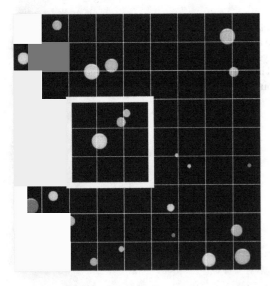

Figure 7-5. Just check for collisions between sprites in the same collsision zone

So instead of checking for a collision between the big white circle and the 24 other circles on the screen, we just need to check for a collision between it and the 2 smaller circles in the upper-right area of the collision zone. That's reduced the number of collision checks by about 90%!

And that's all there is to it! But how you can actually create a spatial grid system like this in code and use it in a game?

Implementing a Spatial Grid

Run the spatialGrid.html file in this chapter's source files for a working example. It's a simple marble-flicking game. Select a marble with the mouse, drag, and release. Watch as the marble bounces around the screen and collides with other marbles, as shown in Figure 7-6.

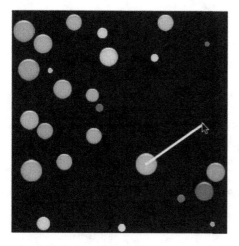

Figure 7-6. *Click, drag, and release to watch the marbles bounce around the screen*

Take a look at the complete source code for details on how this little game prototype works. For our purposes, we're just interested in how the spatial grid collision system works. But, there are two things you need to know about code that we're going to look at ahead:

- It all runs inside the game loop, so it's updated on every frame.

- All the circle sprites are referenced in an array called `marbles.children`.

Ok, got it? Now let's look at the code!

Coding the Spatial Grid

The first thing we need to do is create the grid. This is just a 2D array with cells that match the number of rows and columns we want for our grid. The array is first initialized with empty elements. Then, the code loops through all the sprites and uses our good old `getIndex` function to insert them in to their correct cells, based on each sprite's x/y pixel coordinates. Our code does all this inside a function called `spatialGrid`, which lets you specify the size of the grid and size of each cell, in pixels.

```
let spatialGrid = (widthInPixels, heightInPixels, cellSizeInPixels, spritesArray) => {

  //Find out how many cells we need and how long the
  //grid array should be
  let width = widthInPixels / cellSizeInPixels,
    height = heightInPixels / cellSizeInPixels,
    length = width * height;

  //Initialize an empty grid
  let gridArray = [];

  //Add empty sub-arrays to the element
  for (let i = 0; i < length; i++) {

    //Add empty arrays to each element. This is where
    //we're going to store sprite references
    gridArray.push([]);
  }

  //Add the sprites to the grid
  spritesArray.forEach(sprite => {

    //Find out the sprite's current map index position
    let index = getIndex(sprite.x, sprite.y, cellSizeInPixels, cellSizeInPixels, width);

    //Add the sprite to the array at that index position
    gridArray[index].push(sprite);
  });

  //Return the array
  return gridArray;
};

//Create the spatial grid and add the marble sprites to it
let grid = spatialGrid(512, 512, 64, marbles.children);
```

We now have a 2D array called grid. Each sub-array it contains will either be empty, or contain references to sprites in a way that matches the positions of the sprites on the screen. For example, you might have an array that looks like this:

```
[
  [],[circle1],[],[],[],[],[],[circle2],[],
  [circle3],[],[circle4],[circle5],[],[],[],[],[],
  [],[],[],[],[],[],[],[],[circle6],
  [],[],[],[circle7],[circle8],[],[],[],[],
  [],[circle9],[],[circle10],[],[circle11],[],[],[],
  [circle12, circle13],[],[],[],[],[],[circle14],[circle15],[],
  [circle16],[circle17],[],[],[],[circle18],[],[],[],
  [],[],[circle19],[],[],[circle20],[],[],[circle21],
  [],[circle20],[circle23],[],[],[],[],[circle24],[circle25]
]
```

(The actual names of the sprites, such as `circle1` and `circle2`, are just for illustrative purposes – those names are not actually produced by the code.)

Figure 7-7 shows how this array compares to the screen positions of the same sprites.

```
[
 [],[circle1],[],[],[],[],[],[circle2],[],
 [circle3],[],[circle4],[circle5],[],[],[],[],[],
 [],[],[],[],[],[],[],[],[circle6],
 [],[],[],[circle7],[circle8],[],[],[],[],
 [],[circle9],[],[circle10],[],[circle11],[],[],[],
 [circle12, circle13],[],[],[],[],[],[circle14],[circle15],[],
 [circle16],[circle17],[],[],[],[circle18],[],[],[],
 [],[],[circle19],[],[],[circle20],[],[],[circle21],
 [],[circle20],[circle23],[],[],[],[],[circle24],[circle25]
]
```

Figure 7-7. *The sprites are positioned in the array to match their screen positions*

In a game with densely packed sprites, you might have many cells that hold references to more than one sprite.

The next step is to loop through all the sprites and find out whether there are any other sprites in its collision zone. (Remember, the collision zone is the eight cells surrounding the sprite, plus the cell that the sprite itself occupies.) If there are any sprites in the collision zone, the code does a narrowphase collision check using a custom function called `movingCircleCollision` to bounce the sprites apart (see *Foundation Game Design with HTML5 and JavaScript* (Apress, 2012) for details on how `movingCircleCollision` works.) Finally, the current sprite being checked is removed from the `grid` array because all its possible collisions have been checked and we want to prevent other sprites from trying to recheck it in a later iteration of the loop.

```
//Loop through all the sprites
for (let i = 0; i < marbles.children.length; i++) {

  //Get a reference to the current sprite in the loop
  let sprite = marbles.children[i];

  //Find out the sprite's current map index position
  let gridWidthInTiles = 512 / 64;
  let index = getIndex(sprite.x, sprite.y, 64, 64, gridWidthInTiles);

  //Find out what the surrounding cells contain, including those that
  //might be beyond the borders of the grid
  let allSurroundingCells = [
    grid[index - gridWidthInTiles - 1],
    grid[index - gridWidthInTiles],
    grid[index - gridWidthInTiles + 1],
    grid[index - 1],
    grid[index],
    grid[index + 1],
    grid[index + gridWidthInTiles - 1],
    grid[index + gridWidthInTiles],
    grid[index + gridWidthInTiles + 1]
  ];
```

```
//Find all the sprites that might be colliding with this current sprite
for (let j = 0; j < allSurroundingCells.length; j++) {

    //Get a reference to the current surrounding cell
    let cell = allSurroundingCells[j]

    //If the cell isn't `undefined` (beyond the grid borders)
    //and it's not empty, check for a collision between
    //the current sprite and sprites in the cell
    if (cell && cell.length !== 0) {

        //Loop through all the sprites in the cell
        for (let k = 0; k < cell.length; k++) {

            //Get a reference to the current sprite being checked
            //in the cell
            let surroundingSprite = cell[k];

            //If the sprite in the cell is not the same as the current
            //sprite in the main loop, then check for a collision
            //between those sprites
            if (surroundingSprite !== sprite) {

                //Perform a narrow-phase collision check to bounce
                //the sprites apart
                g.movingCircleCollision(sprite, surroundingSprite);
            }
        }
    }
}

//Finally, remove this current sprite from the current
//spatial grid cell because all possible collisions
//involving this sprite have been checked
grid[index] = grid[index].filter(x => x !== sprite);
}
```

And that's all there is to it! By doing an efficient broadphase check first, and then only doing a performance-heavy narrowphase check if there's a likelihood of a collision, we've greatly increased the efficiency of our collision system.

Why does this code use old-fashioned `for` loops, instead of more sleek and modern `forEach` loops? `for` loops tend to be ever so slightly more efficient. Usually, the difference is not enough to favor `for` loops in general, but because collision detection is one of the most performance-demanding tasks your games will be doing, using a `for` loop in this context will usually win you a small performance boost.

Other Broadphase Collision Strategies

A spatial grid is an excellent all-purpose broadphase collision-detection system that is a game designer's staple. It's hard to be beat for simplicity, speed and low overhead. However, there are many other broadphase collision strategies that each has its unique take on the problem. Here are the four most popular:

- **Hierarchical grid**: In a fixed-sized spatial grid such as the one we've been using in this chapter, the cell size must be as large as the largest object. But what if you have a game with a few very big objects and a lot of very small objects? The cell size will need to be big enough to accommodate those large objects, even if there aren't very many of them. You'll end up with a situation where each cell is full of many small objects, each doing expensive distance checks against one another. A hierarchical grid solves this possible problem by creating two or more grids of different-sized cells. It creates a grid with big cells for the big objects, and another one for the small objects, and any range of differing cell size grids in between. Collision checks between small objects are handled in the small-cell grid, and collisions between big objects are handled in the big-cell grid. If a small object needs to check for a collision with a big object, the system checks the cells that correspond to both grids.

- **Quadtree**: A specific type of hierarchical grid. The game world is divided into 4 rectangles, which are in turn divided into 4 more rectangles, resulting in 16. Each of those 16 rectangles is again split into 4 smaller rectangles, and this continues depending on how much detail you need. Each of the smaller rectangles is a child of the larger parents. The quadtree system figures out which objects to test for collisions depending on their level in their hierarchy. The 3D version of the quadtree is called an octree.

- **Sort and sweep**: Sort the objects in arrays based on their x and y positions. Check for overlaps on the x and y axes and, if found, do a more precise distance check. Because the objects are spatially sorted first, likely collision candidates come to the forefront first.

- **BSP tree**: Space is partitioned in a way that closely matches the geometry of the game objects. It's useful because it means that the partitions can be used both for collisions and to define environmental boundaries. Binary space partitioning (BSP) trees are closely related to quadtrees, but they're more versatile. BSP trees are widely used in collision detection for 3D games.

I suggest that you spend some time researching these other broadphase collision strategies. You may find one of them holds a particularly good solution to a complex collision problem you might be facing.

The definitive reference text on collision for games is Christer Ericson's classic Real Time Collision Detection (Morgan Kaufman, 2004.) Although the source code examples are written in C++ (a close relative of JavaScript), the algorithms can be adapted for any programming language or technical implementation.

But remember: don't try and preemptively optimize your collision system before you need to! If your game runs fine on all your target platforms without needing to use a spatial grid or a quadtree just leave it alone – it's fine!

Summary

In this chapter you've learned how you can add hidden game information in arrays, and use that information to add a richness and complexity to your game world. The AI race car showed you how, with minimal, easy code, you can create a game entity that behaves in a complex, intelligent, and unpredictable way. You also learned how to create and use the best all-purpose and low-overhead broadphase collision strategy: the spatial grid. Using a spatial grid dramatically reduces the number of collision checks your games will need to do, and it's easy to modify and tweak to your needs.

And, we've reached the end of the book! You've now got all the skills you need to start making a wide variety of 2D action games in any genre. From level design, to collision detection to pathfinding and the amazing efficiency of tile-based architecture, you've now mastered all the game designer's classic techniques. Now go and make some great games!

Index

© Rex van der Spuy 2017
R. van der Spuy, *The Advanced Game Developer's Toolkit*, DOI 10.1007/978-1-4842-1097-0

■ V, W, X, Y, Z

Get the eBook for only $5!

Why limit yourself?

With most of our titles available in both PDF and ePUB format, you can access your content wherever and however you wish—on your PC, phone, tablet, or reader.

Since you've purchased this print book, we are happy to offer you the eBook for just $5.

To learn more, go to http://www.apress.com/companion or contact support@apress.com.

Apress®

Printed in the United States
By Bookmasters